CW01197243

SHETLAND FOLK-LORE

BY

JOHN SPENCE, F.E.I.S.

Facsimile reprint 1999
Llanerch Publishers
Felinfach
ISBN 1 86143 085 X

LERWICK
JOHNSON & GREIG
1899

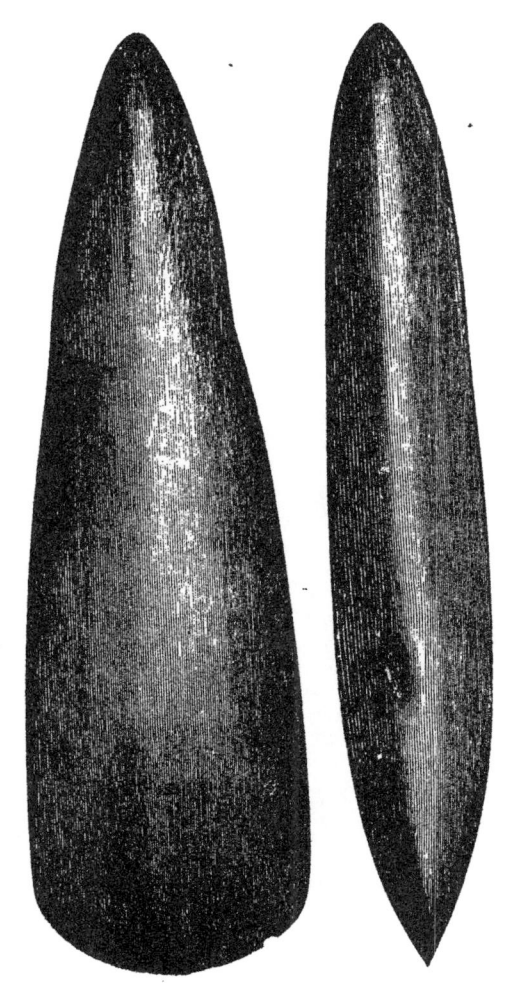

FIG. 1.—*Polished Stone Axe.*

SHETLAND FOLK-LORE

PRINTED BY
JOHNSON AND GREIG, LERWICK

TO

EVERY LOVER OF THE "OLD ROCK"

THIS VOLUME IS

RESPECTFULLY DEDICATED

BY THE AUTHOR

All Rights Reserved

PREFACE

THERE is undoubtedly a growing tendency among the younger people of the present day to undervalue or neglect what has come down to us from former times. The object of this work is to preserve the memory of the old traditions, stories, phrases, words, and social customs, which were once familiar to bygone generations of our island folk. Most of the tales that constitute the folk-lore of our islands have a charm of their own. To understand that charm fully, one must picture to one's self the old grandfather or grandmother telling to the eager bairns, round the blazing peat fire on the long winter evenings, tales of *trows* and witches, spirits and apparitions, until at last the children

Preface

who had gathered from the neighbouring houses felt afraid to venture back alone. These traditionary tales formed virtually the only current literature the people had. In those times information was conveyed by tale and story, and not by books as now. To save the relics of the past and interest the rising generation in them, one must use the printed page. The young folk do not listen now; they read.

For nearly forty years the writer has been gathering from the lips of the old folk the sayings and superstitions handed down to them. This volume is the outcome of his gleanings in that field. Though it does not profess to be exhaustive, it is placed before the public as the first book specially devoted to the subject. It thus contains the fullest collection of Shetland folk-lore available to students of the subject and to natives of the Islands at home and abroad. The book may chance to have, as well, some value for philologists. The dialect of the

Preface

Islands has been largely used throughout to give the necessary local colouring, but the author thinks that this will not cause the southern reader any very serious difficulty, as in most cases explanations of the words have been supplied. If the writer succeeds in interesting those who take pleasure in recalling the old times and the old manners, and in stimulating any of his readers to join in the work of rescuing our island traditions ere they fade away into obscurity, he will consider himself amply rewarded.

The author desires here to acknowledge his indebtedness to James M. Goudie, Esq., Lerwick, for valuable assistance rendered in writing the chapter on "Prehistoric Remains"; and to the Rev. Thomas Mathewson, Lerwick, and J. J. Haldane Burgess, Esq., M.A., Lerwick, for many helpful suggestions and much assistance given while the book was passing through the press.

The author has to record his thanks to

Preface

Edward Stanford, Esq., London, for the permission given to reproduce the illustration of the Shetland *sixern*; and to Dr. Joseph Anderson, on behalf of the Society of Antiquaries, for the use of the remaining woodcuts which appear in this volume.

JOHN SPENCE.

THE SCHOOLHOUSE,
  VASSA, SHETLAND,
    September, 1899.

'CONTENTS

	PAGE
THE PICTS AND THEIR BROCHS .	17
First inhabitants of Shetland . . .	17
Finns, The	18
Magic powers of	20
Legends of	22
Picts, The	27
Cultivation of land by . . .	29
Mode of fishing	32
Plundered by the Norsemen . .	34
Brochs	35
Dwelling-places of	37
Battle fought in Unst . . .	40
Conquered by the Norsemen . .	42
Brochs in Nesting	44
In Unst	46
In Sandness	52
In Shetland	57
PREHISTORIC REMAINS . . .	61
Stone Age	62

Contents

PREHISTORIC REMAINS (continued)— PAGE
   Rude Stone Implements 63
   Polished Stone Implements. . . . 66
   Shetland Wooded in Early Times . . 69
   Perforated Stone Axes. 74
   Stone Knives 76
   Domestic Utensils of Stone. . . . 77
   Burial Mounds 78
   Cinerary Urns 81
   Standing Stones : 89
   Stone Circles 91
   Sculptured Stones 94
   Runic Stones 100
   Bronze Weapons 102
   Bronze Ornaments 105

FOLK-LORE 109
   Sea and Weather Lore 110
   The Haf Fishing 124
   Trows and Witches 139
   Social Life in Olden Times . . . 169
   Festivities 187

PROVERBS AND SAYINGS . . . 205

THE LAMMAS FOY 235

INDEX

ILLUSTRATIONS

		PAGE
1. Polished Stone Axe, found at Tingwall— *Frontispiece*		
2. Rude Stone Implement, found at Watsness, Walls	.	64
3. Club-like Handled Implement of Sandstone, found at Burrafirth, Unst	.	65
4. Polished Stone Axe, found at Tingwall	.	71
5. Polished Axe of Porphyrite, found at Mount Braa, near Lerwick	.	73
6. Sculptured Stone from Churchyard of Papil, Burra Isle	.	95
7. Spear Head of Bronze, found at Lunnasting		103
8. Oval Bowl-shaped Brooch of Bronze, found at Clibberswick, Unst	.	105
9. Trefoil-shaped Brooch of Bronze, from Unst	.	106
10. Shetland Sixern (six-oared boat)	.	125
11. Shetland Quern or Hand-Mill	.	171
12. Shetland Water-Mill	.	173
13. Shetland Kollie (fish-oil lamp)	.	198

THE PICTS AND THEIR BROCHS

The plee o' the skorie, the birr o' the snipe,
The roar o' the burn, an' the swill o' the stripe,
The sough o' the nort' wind, the töve o' the sea—
Such music, dear "Old Rock," is heard best in thee.

THE PICTS AND THEIR BROCHS

THE first inhabitants of Shetland, who were they, and whence did they come? are questions wrapped in obscurity; and although much has been said and written on the subject, it has never been advanced beyond the stage of conjecture. It is generally admitted that the Picts were the first inhabitants of Shetland, and that they came from Scotland, but from what region they migrated thither is a subject of uncertainty.

It is reasonable to suppose that the

Shetland Folk-Lore

earlier migrations of the human race have been from east to west—hence we may infer that the people called Picts were Finnish adventurers from the Scandinavian peninsula, who migrated or were driven westward about the beginning of or shortly before the Christian era. And as Shetland is the nearest land to Norway, they probably colonised these islands first, and in time proceeded westward by way of the Orkneys to the mainland of Scotland. In support of this view it may be mentioned that there are a few place-names in which the Finns appear to be commemorated, *e.g.*, Finnigirt and Finnie, in the Island of Fetlar; and Finnister, in Nesting, etc. It is worthy of note that these places are associated in the public mind with trolls, or at least something uncanny. Of Finnigirt Dr. Jacobsen says: "There are a few legends told about places along this dyke stead, and the spot where it terminates on the south side of the island has been of old a noted place for trolls."

The Picts and their Brochs

Regarding Finnister in Nesting, the name is applied to one of the numerous *punds* or enclosures found in the Shetland scattalds. The ground inside the old Finnister dyke had evidently been a *toon*, and had been occupied as a croft. It is traditionally said that the last family all died or mysteriously disappeared by some enchantment, and although the ground is the richest spot in the pasture, no animal was said to remain on it after sundown.

In the parish of Delting there is a green hillock called "Finnister Knowe," probably a burial mound. Also at Brettabister, in the parish of Nesting, near a large Pictish ruin, there is a place called the "Finnie Knowe," *i.e.*, the Finns' Knoll; and the same name is applied to a green hillock near the burn of Grunafirth. And further, there is in a remote glen between the hill of Boofell and the Lang Kame two little hillocks called Finnister Hadds. The word *hadd* is applied particularly to the hole made by a burrowing animal.

Even the earth dwelling of man might be termed a *hadd* or hiding-place. Hence the name would signify the Finns' burrow or hiding-place. Earth houses have existed in the neighbourhood, remains of which may still be seen.

It is also worthy of note that there were, and even yet linger, numerous legends in Shetland which may be regarded as of Finnish origin, or at least associated in the minds of old Shetlanders with real or imaginary beings whom they called Finns. There were persons supposed to be descendants of Finns, who were accredited with extraordinary powers. They could render themselves visible or invisible at pleasure. They could metamorphose themselves into the likeness of beast, bird, or fish. It is even said that they could assume the appearance of a beetle, hence we have to this day the *witchie-clock* and the *tur-diel*, two kinds of beetles. They were supposed to understand the language of the *corbies* or ravens, and this

The Picts and their Brochs

gift often proved to be of considerable advantage. An old man possessed of this Finnish art had lost a young horse. He wandered up hill and down dale for several days without finding the straying animal, but one morning two *corbies* alighted on a knoll near his house and engaged in a short croaking dialogue, and to his surprise the conversation was interpreted as follows:—

> *1st Corbie*—Dead horse! dead horse!
> *2nd Corbie*—Whaar pairt? whaar pairt?
> *1st Corbie*—Upo da Neep, upo da Neep.
> *2nd Corbie*—Is he fat? is he fat?
> *1st Corbie*—Aa spick, aa spick.

The man, on going to the place indicated in the *corbies'* speech, found that his own horse had fallen over the *banks*.

Persons who were possessed of the Finnish art could perform feats by sea or water quite impossible to ordinary mortals. They could raise the wind like furies in order to wreck the crafts of their enemies, and change the storm into a calm.

Shetland Folk-Lore

The following are the words of an ancient spell for *laying* the wind at sea:

> "Robin cam ow'r da vaana wi' da sköna
> Twaabie, toobie, keelikim, koolikim,
> Pattrik alanks da Robin,
> Gude runk da gro."

A Finn man could cross from Norwick in Unst to Bergen in Norway and return between the hours of sunset and sunrise, the traditional speed being nine miles to the *warp* (stroke of the oar). They were adepts at recovering things lost in the sea which to ordinary mortals were irrecoverable.

A story is told in Unst of a Finn whose two sons had a winter boat. They had been off at the handline, and on their return one evening after dark were recounting the day's adventures to the old man. Among other things they mentioned their ill-luck in being fast to *da baldin* (*i.e.*, a turbot) which had broken a *skoag* that the father had prepared. A little later he told them to put on the

The Picts and their Brochs

supper, as he was going out for a short time, and would be back by the time the kettle was "poor'd." Well, just as the supper was ready the guidman entered the house, bearing on his back a large turbot, in the mouth of which hung the lost *skoag*. Says one of the boys: "Guid be naar dee, daa, whaar's du been aa dis?" "Aks du dat," says the old man; and, throwing down the fish, he exclaims: "Ill stjund ta dy glyed face. I haed da Öra at da Ötsta wi' Vytaberg at Tonga afore I made up wi' 'im."

The Finns were said to be the only beings who could safely ride the *Neugle*. The *neugle* or *nicker* was a water deity that appeared in the form of a sleek horse, having an erect mane and tail like the "rim o' a muckle wheel." He frequented the banks of burns and the margins of lonely lakes, playing his pranks on watermills (where the owner had neglected to give him an offering) by stopping the tirl. If any luckless nocturnal wanderer, mis-

Shetland Folk-Lore

taking the *neugle* for a real horse, should get astride the uncanny beast, he was at once borne with the swiftness of an arrow into the middle of the nearest lake or dam, and there left struggling in the water, while he beheld the creature rushing towards the opposite shore like a streak of *mareel*. It is not said that anyone was ever actually drowned by the *neugle*. But the Finns could ride the water horse, and were supposed to utilise him in some of their rapid movements.

In Shetland folk-lore the Finns, both men and women, were supposed to possess a skin or garment like the covering of a *selkie* (seal). Enrobed in this magic coat, they could take to the water as readily and as safely as an amphibious animal. But if by any mischance they lost or were deprived of it, then the rest of their days must be spent on *terra firma* like other ordinary mortals.

In old times there was an aversion to and superstitious dread of killing a *selkie*,

The Picts and their Brochs

lest it should be a metamorphic Finn; and in the case of a gun being aimed at it, the weapon was sure to miss fire until a piece of silver money was placed above the shot.

A story is told of a Norway Finn that fell in love with a bonny lass of the ordinary rank. But her father refused to sanction the union. The Finnish lover, not to be deprived of the object of his ardent affection, succeeded in carrying her off in his boat. The father, being apprised of the elopement, gave chase with all possible speed. The Finn, on seeing that he was pursued, put the helm into the hand of his fair lady, while he cut chips off the shank of the oar and threw them overboard. These, falling into the water, appeared like boats to the onlooker, and the lady's father, seeing the runaway craft escorted by a whole fleet, gave up the chase.

Even in recent times persons who were marked as being particularly lucky, and those who were supposed to be skilled in the Black Art, were spoken of as Norway Finns. And a person whose odd, eccentric appearance and actions would lead to the supposition that "they could dö mair dan maet demsels," was termed a *Hjokfinnie body*—*i.e.*, a buried Finn up again.

The words or charms that were used by persons who professed the healing art, such as "telling oot" toothache or ringworm, casting the *aaba knot* or tying the *wrestin treed*, sometimes had reference to Finns, *e.g.* :

"A Finn cam ow'r frae Noraway
Ta pit töthake awa,
Oot o' da flesh an' oot o' da bane,
Oot o' da sinin an' inta da skin,
Oot o' da skin an' inta da stane,
An' dere may du remain."

These are a few of the Finn legends found in Shetlandic story, and it is difficult to understand how such stories came to exist unless a people called Finns had had a long-standing connection with the

The Picts and their Brochs

islands, either as an independent people, prior to the Norse invasion, or accompanying the Norse warriors at a later date.

But to return to the Picts. Whoever they were, they are gone, leaving nothing behind them but the numerous brochs, burial mounds, and standing stones; and as we gaze on these mouldering remains of a byegone age, we can only soliloquise in the words of the poet:

> "Once in the flight of ages past
> There lived a man, and who was he?
> Unknown the region of his birth,
> The land in which he died unknown.
> His name has perished from the earth,
> This truth survives alone:
> That joy and grief, and hope and fear,
> Alternate triumphed in his breast;
> His bliss and woe—
> A smile—a tear—
> Oblivion hides the rest."

The Picts probably occupied the islands for a thousand years. They have been a numerous, industrious, and intelligent

Shetland Folk-Lore

people, inhabiting the land from end to end, as these remains show. Upwards of a hundred brochs and other remains may be traced in Shetland. Their number may be gathered from the many place-names to which they have given birth. In every parish there are townships called Brough, while other derivations are common, such as Burra, Burravoe, Burrafirth, Burragarth, Burraland, Burgalea, Burgasand, Burgawater, etc., etc. Then we have a great many names that take the broch as a suffix, *e.g.*, Collingsbrough, Footabrough, Gossabrough, Overbrough, Snaabrough, Strandiebrough, Railsbrough, Musselbrough (at Uyeasound), etc., etc.

There are at least ten brochs in Unst, viz., Balta, Balliasta, Burrafirth, Oganess, Colvidale, Newgord Holm, Uyeasound, Underhool, Woodwick, and Snaabrough; and there are almost as many in Yell, while Fetlar possesses at least three. There are four existing brochs in Delting, eight in Northmavine, and, in the districts

The Picts and their Brochs

of Sandness and Aithsting there are traces of no less than nine brochs, several of which have been important structures of their kind. There are three brochs in Whalsay, and in South Nesting district within a radius of two miles no less than six Pictish ruins may be found. And similarly all over the southern mainland, the utmost limit of which (Sumburgh Head) derives its name from these ancient remains.

As to how the Picts supported themselves, we must be left a good deal to conjecture. Their means of livelihood were no doubt very precarious, drawn chiefly from the sheep and cattle that pastured on the hills. They perhaps grew corn, which they made into meal by pounding in a stone mortar, the old *knockin' stane* and *mell*—now obsolete—being an improvement on the original. Some ancient people, presumably the Picts, have occupied the pastures and outruns of Shetland in a manner never subsequently attempted.

Shetland Folk-Lore

All the hills and outruns of the islands are ramified by a network of the remains of old stone dykes. Those vestiges (which seldom have any name) are very ancient, probably coeval with the brochs. There is a place in Unst, near the broch of Underhool, where what appears to be the outer dyke of an old town can be traced; but for a considerable distance the mark of the stead was lost to view, and I concluded that the dyke had either never existed or the stones had been removed. But what was my surprise, on returning after many years' absence, to find that the crofters, on cutting the ground for peats, had uncovered the whole length of the old dyke, leaving it almost entire, after being buried for centuries under four feet of peat moss.

Since I am referring to these ancient enclosures, I may mention that a short time ago, while a party of workmen were engaged in the construction of a road inside this old dyke, a burial place was

The Picts and their Brochs

discovered, in which were found three graves, each enclosed by four rough stone slabs. No human remains were found, but each cist contained a mortar and a lamp, both of stone. The mortar was smaller than the old *knockin' stane*, and by its shape and wear seemed adapted for holding between the knees of the operator when being used. The inside hollow was capable of holding two pounds of meal. The lamp, as I shall call it, was a bit of stone hollowed out like a saucer—just a stone *collie*. It looked as if it had been saturated with oil, and bore traces of the action of fire.

These were probably Pictish remains, and though perhaps of very little archæological interest, yet tell in unmistakable language that the Picts, like ourselves, looked upon the grave as a darksome journey, and, like us, felt the need of some provision for the great hereafter. Hence, according to the light they possessed, the *collie* and the *knockin' stane* were the most likely to supply those wants.

The Picts drew their means of support not only from the pastures and their scanty agricultural productions, but then, as now, the "harvest of the sea" contributed largely to their support.

Their mode of fishing was no doubt of the most primitive kind, particularly rock fishing—or *craigs*. The extent to which this mode of fishing has been practised in Shetland may be gathered from the vast number of small round holes, hollowed out by human hands, and known as "the cup holes." All round the islands, unless where the height or nature of the cliffs render it impossible, these holes are found; and not one, to my knowledge, is met with in a situation unsuitable for a *craigasoad* or *bersit* (rock seat). I have sometimes landed on parts of the coast now little frequented, and have been surprised to find a nicely formed cup hole, and could trace, by the wear on the stone, where the

The Picts and their Brochs

ancient craigsman had sat, where his feet had stood, and where his *böddie* had hung. These holes are not often met with on the low shores of our inland voes, because there the primitive boat of the period could fish in ordinary weather.

Several conjectures have been made as to the origin and use of those ancient marks. Some have supposed that they have been used in connection with worship. I do not believe that those who made them were so foolish as to climb the heights of Tukkabersoada or Lucegrood, or descend to the Bersit o' Millyague to offer their devotions.

It is commonly supposed that these holes were formed for the purpose of pounding and holding *rooder* for *soe*, or lure. Probably this latter theory contains an element of truth. The *craig* fisherman would have found the cup hole very convenient for holding bait, and no doubt he utilised it for that purpose while engaged in fishing. The bait, I imagine, was lim-

Shetland Folk-Lore

pets, and these were not prepared either as bait or lure by crushing or bruising, but by chewing in the mouth; and I presume the Picts were as expert as we are in the art of chewing, and far in advance of us in chewing apparatus.

The *craigstane* or *bexsit* was to the ancient dweller of our islands what the fishing boat is to the modern fisherman. They were among his most valuable possessions, supplying him with the means of subsistence when other sources were exhausted. May we not suppose that those old marks were originally intended to give the maker some sort of proprietary right to that particular *craigsitting* (as they are sometimes called), and would probably descend from father to son?

Now, while the Picts were living peacefully among the hills and round the voes and creeks of Shetland,—tending their sheep, cultivating plots in sheltered nooks, brewing their heather beer, gathering shell-fish and birds' eggs in their season

The Picts and their Brochs

to eke out and add variety to their dietary,—suddenly their quiet is broken by strangers landing on the coast. Those unwelcome visitors were Norsemen, who made piratical expeditions to almost all parts of European waters. The poverty of their country induced those sea rovers, or Vikings, to adopt this course; and also their religion inspired them with a love for daring enterprise, since it taught them that warriors fallen in battle were admitted into all the joys of Valhalla. The Picts soon discovered that the strangers who had landed on their shores were bent on plunder, with perhaps an eye to settlement and the acquisition of territory.

Now, those first visitors would doubtless leave after a short sojourn, carrying off such booty as they could obtain, and this would at once suggest to the Pictish mind the necessity for some means of defence; and with the instinct of self-preservation and the love of home, they would at once take steps to fortify themselves against the raids of the invaders. Hence the construction of the numerous brochs or castles to which we have referred. The mass of stone, often transported from a distance, used in some of the brochs is something marvellous, and points to the concerted action of a multitude of hands. The sites chosen were such as could best facilitate the transmission of messages by means of signals from end to end of the land with almost telegraphic speed. It is noticeable that from one broch another can be seen, and from this a third, and so on, from Scaw to Fitful. If a broch can be found that does not fulfil this condition, a *voard* or *wart*, which signifies a watch-tower, is in the neighbourhood.

The most favoured sites for brochs were holms in lochs, holms and skerries near the seashore, especially such holms, or islets, as were wholly or partially connected with the mainland by tidal beaches or reefs; and where such formation was absent, a sort of half-tide footway, or *brig*,

The Picts and their Brochs

was built, sometimes in a zig-zag direction, intended to mislead the stranger who should attempt to find the submerged path

The doorways and passages of the brochs were generally so low as not to allow an ordinary person to walk erect in them, and this has probably led to the popular belief that the Picts, or *Pechts*, as they are commonly called, were a dwarfish race. But it does not necessarily follow that they were such. The low formation was intended to add to the security of their abode. They could easily and instinctively accommodate themselves to the size of their own familiar surroundings whereas a stranger would be unable to make his way through such contracted openings with anything like speed; and further, a narrow passage could be more easily defended than a wide entrance.

The Picts also constructed earth houses remains of which have been found both on hillsides and in level fields: on House field, at Norwick; at Fyall, near Harolds

Shetland Folk-Lore

wick; at Scraefield, in Balliasta; and at the foot of Saxaford Hill, near the Noup of Burrafirth. Those subterranean dwellings or hiding-places are more numerous than we are apt to imagine. There are three places near the seashore north of Scuddleswick, in Nesting, where, I believe, the remains of this class of dwelling may be seen. A great mass of stones in a small, cup-like hollow where the ground is very deep can only be accounted for as fallen-in earth houses. One of these has been a sort of double circle something like the figure 8; and in the neighbourhood are two burial mounds, viz., at the burn of Scuddleswick and the burn of Whinalea.

Natural caves and *hellyers* along the sea coast were no doubt used by those early inhabitants as places of retreat. The names of some of these, together with legends connected with them, lead to this conclusion. For example, the Hellyer o' Fivlagord, the Den o' Pettasmog, the Hole o' Henkie, and the Ha' o' Doon

The Picts and their Brochs

Hellyer, are places that from time immemorial have been associated in the public mind with *trows* or *hillfolk*. The names *Fivla* and *Tivla* appear to have been favourite appellations given to *trows* of the feminine gender, and are often met with in fairy legends (see Jacobsen's "Shetland Dialect," p. 69). The word *fivla* is used in Unst in designating a light fall of snow. Just as much as can give to the ground a wierd, silver-grey appearance is called a "fivla o' snaa." *Henk* is applied to the movements of trolls, particularly in a fairy dance. Old people spoke of having seen numbers of puny beings dancing round a *fairy knowe*. These were spoken of as a "scrae o' henkies." A fairy wife who failed to obtain a partner in a dance was heard to express herself thus:

"'Hey!' co (quoth) Cuttie; an 'ho!' co Cuttie;
'An' wha 'ill dance wi' me?' co Cuttie.
Shö luked aboot an' saw naebody;
'Sae I'll henk awa mesel',' co Cuttie."

Shetland Folk-Lore

The Picts, having constructed their brochs or castles, would no doubt have a trusty sentinel located in each and on the neighbouring *voard*, where he might be seen gazing out on the mysterious ocean. If, perchance, his eyes descry a suspicious craft in the offing, he at once sets fire to a heap of dry heather kept in readiness for the purpose, and in less time than it takes to read this page the brochs are ablaze, and the inhabitants from Scaw to Sumburgh are warned of the impending danger. Those who cannot fight flock to the caves, *hellyers*, and earth houses, while every broch is garrisoned with brave men and true, determined to repel the invaders. Tradition speaks of several battles as having taken place. A great battle is said to have been fought at Norwick in Unst, and also one in the neighbourhood of the Blue Mull. The Outer Mull is a sort of Gibraltar-like formation, and across the narrow neck of land between Infraneb and Fraeklesgeo there is the remains of

The Picts and their Brochs

a great earthwork called "the Virkie." In this fortress the Picts no doubt entrenched themselves, and would be able to offer stern resistance to the Norsemen. An old township near the traditional battlefield is called Viggie, which is said to signify a place of conflict. A story was told in Unst, how the ground in Blue Mull was subsequently cultivated, but had to be given up, owing to the stalks of corn being filled with blood, supposed to be a judgment on account of the carnage that had taken place there. The stone implements called celts, known popularly as *thunderbolts*, are generally believed to have been Pictish weapons of warfare, and the places where they are found are supposed to have been old battlefields. Few of such implements have, as far as I know, been found in any of the brochs. Some of them are very rude, others finely shaped and beautifully polished, and it is likely that they were also used for domestic purposes.

Shetland Folk-Lore

But the fierce, warlike Norsemen came from time to time in greater numbers, and were more than a match for the Picts, who, worn out in their vain struggle and weakened by frequent losses, at last yielded to the conquerors. Whether they were absorbed with the incomers, or left the islands to seek a home elsewhere, or were totally extirpated, it is impossible to tell. Tradition points to the last theory. It is said that a few were spared to teach the art of brewing an intoxicating beer from heather, but rather than divulge the secret they let themselves be slain. But we can scarcely believe that the Norsemen put to death the women and children. After the din of war had ceased, the new settlers would probably get glimpses in the early morning or grey moonlight of the earth house dwellers still surviving in their midst, clinging to their old haunts with that tenacious love of home and offspring that characterises the human race; and probably those of us who pride ourselves

The Picts and their Brochs

as being descended from the old Vikings may add to our boast by claiming to have a blending of Pictish blood in our veins.

There are a few place-names in Shetland that may be regarded as commemorative of the Pictish occupation, such as Pettasmog, which Dr. Jacobsen regards as signifying the hiding-place of the Picts. Then there is Pettaster in Unst, Pettigarth in Whalsay, Pettafirth in Bressay, and Pettadale and Pettawater in Nesting. In olden times Pettadale was spoken of as the chief haunt of *trows* or *hillfolk*. To pass Pettawater alone after nightfall required an extraordinary nerve. On the top of the hill overlooking this lonely lake there is a cup-shaped hollow, like the crater of an extinct volcano, called Da Byre o' Hookame, probably from being used as a hiding-place for cattle.

I shall now add a few descriptive notes with reference to some of the brochs, particularly with reference to those that have escaped public notice.

Shetland Folk-Lore

There are several brochs in Nesting, to two of which I shall briefly refer. The Broch of Railsbrough, situated on a small islet or skerry at the east side of Catfirth Voe, appears to have been a building unique of its kind; at anyrate, it is different from any broch I have seen. I examined it about twenty years ago while the stones were being removed for building purposes. It consisted of one circular wall about twenty feet in diameter. I do not think it had been chambered, as the wall did not appear to be very thick—say about four feet. The enclosed circular space was divided into quadrants by four walls meeting at right angles in the centre, like a cross within a circle; and in the centre, at the point where the four walls met, there stood a standing-stone six or seven feet high. These inner walls had been very thin, not more than twelve inches thick, and were built of small stones. A doorway on the east side of the outer wall led into one of the inside compartments, but whether there was internal access to all the four divisions, I am unable to tell. The islet on which the broch is built is separated from the shore by a narrow sound, dry at spring tide, and the usual stepping-stones or bridge had been constructed to connect it with the land. Among the ruins were found peat ashes, a stone axe, and a stone lamp similar to that found in the burial mound at Unst. I shall leave the antiquarian reader to conjecture the purpose or design of this building.

The other Nesting broch to which I shall refer claims a little attention. It has no name by which it is known locally, nor does it give a name to any township in the neighbourhood, as is commonly the case. It is situated near the top of the cliffs on a very wild part of the coast, entirely inapproachable from the sea. It has consisted of a centre tower surrounded by two circular walls. The outer wall has been about 220 feet in circumference. The mass of stones used in the building is enormous. The Parish Church of Nesting stands at the base of the broch, and is built wholly of stones taken from the ruin. Yet, notwithstanding this, the heap that remains forms a conical mound measuring about 70 feet in diameter at the base, and 15 feet deep in the centre.

One of the most perfect Pictish strongholds, both on account of its size and also its insular position, is the Broch Holm of Lundawick, in Unst. It is referred to by Hibbert in the following words: "West of the Moul is a rock where are the remains of an ancient burgh, destroyed by time and wilful delapidation." This description is at fault as regards the bearing from the Blue Mull. The broch is E.N.E. from the Mull, and Hibbert's appellation of a "rock" is scarcely fair, for although much diminished in area since the days of Hibbert by the inroads of the sea, yet it can graze a few sheep all the year round.

The Picts and their Brochs

Like all the brochs, time has wasted it, and also wilful delapidation. The laird of Lund built a booth on the Holm with stones taken from the ancient walls, while hundreds of tons have been carried away as ballast by the fleet of *haaf* boats that fished from the Ayre of Newgord. In its original form this must have been one of the most extensive of the brochs. Even in its ruined condition it is sufficiently prominent to be used by fishermen as a landmark at sea for *meithing* (marking) the *Burgascurs*. It is clear that the greater part of the stones required in the construction of this broch have been trans. ported from the mainland, and tradition says that they were quarried in the Gill o' Scraers and shipped to the Holm at the Geo o' Kurkaby. I believe such was not the case, because the Picts were not so un- practical as to fetch stones from a great distance, involving tremendous labour when the same material could be obtained within easy distance. The Gill o' Scraers is a hollow in the side of Vaalafell south of Collister, and distant from the broch about two miles. True, there is a quarry here said to be the broch quarry, but the stones are not of the same kind as those used in the construction of the broch. The stone found in the Scraers quarry is soap-stone, commonly called in Shetland *clamal* or *clebber*. Now, although the stones for the broch were not taken from here according to tradition, yet I shall show what appears to be a relation between this quarry and the true broch quarry. Some years ago, when in this neighbourhood, my attention was drawn to a large hollow in the Brae o' Newgord, a short distance from the shore and right opposite the Broch Holm. The hollow had evidently been a stone quarry, and on enquiry I learned that it locally bore the name of Berg-grave. It was from here, I presume, that the stones for the broch were taken. My reason for this belief rests on the fact that the stone here is of the same nature as that used in the

The Picts and their Brochs

broch, while the name Berg-grave points to the same conclusion; besides, this quarry gives easy access to the Holm—transport downhill. The sound separating the Holm from the shore is here at its narrowest, and shipment could be easily effected at a natural landing place called the Noost o' Kurkaby. Now, in the neighbourhood of the quarry of Berggrave I observed what appeared to be heaps or mounds of débris or refuse of the ancient working; but on removing the green turf by which it was overgrown, I was surprised to find nothing but fragments of soap-stone—the same as is found at Scraers. We are left to conjecture the purpose to be served by the *clamal* from the Gill o' Scraers found at Berg-grave. Perhaps this knowledge might lead to the recovery of a lost art. It should be mentioned that there is a tradition in Unst to the effect that the Picts used *clamal*, or soap-stone, for blasting purposes. Thus it will be observed that the traditions

Shetland Folk-Lore

regarding the stones of this broch may contain an element of truth in a distorted form.

With reference to what is called the "Vir" (*brig*) of the Holm, I am of opinion that it was not formed by the Picts. A built roadway from the Holm to the shore would have involved engineering abilities that we can hardly imagine they possessed. The sound here is several hundred yards in width, and in the middle has a depth of water even at ebb tide sufficient to allow a small vessel to enter. Besides, in wintertime a very heavy ocean swell forces in through this sound—so heavy that no rubble-built wall could resist the impact of the sea. The Picts, being dwellers there and no doubt an observant people, were not likely to undertake a work sure to end in failure. The formation of the Vir is not artificial, but natural. Had it been artificial, the ocean wear of centuries would long ere now have destroyed it; but being natural, it abides, and the cause that

The Picts and their Brochs

produced it being in constant operation, it remains undiminished. Along the line of the Vir two seas meet at right angles, and the result is the formation of a ridge running in a diagonal between the lines of force. The sound here is called Vaarasound. The word Vir appears to be the prefix in the place-name Virkie, in Dunrossness, and of the ancient earthwork in the Blue Mull already referred to.

On the mainland of Unst, half a mile south from the Holm, there is another very extensive broch called the Overbrough, consisting of a central tower with two concentric walls or embankments about 20 feet apart. From this ancient fort a very wide view can be obtained, both seaward and landward. The sentinel on its watch-tower could signal to no fewer than seven brochs, viz.: Brough Holm; Brough of North Yell; Snaabrough, Oganess, and Musselbrough, in Unst; Strandiebrough and Brough Lodge, in Fetlar.

Regarding the brochs in the district of

Shetland Folk-Lore

Sandness my learned friend, the late Mr Robert Jamieson, wrote to me an interesting letter, from which I shall make the following extract:—

"We have several brochs here. The Broch of Easter has been in its day a gigantic building, double walled, chambered like a bee-hive and fitted up with every convenience. About 1840 the laird of Melby used the stones of it in building about three-fourths of a mile of dyke six feet in height, and left as many stones as would build a castle. In the work of excavation, querns, mallets, knives, pottery, and bones of animals, were found, which now would be considered of the greatest value; but unfortunately the workmen knew nothing and cared nothing about the brochs. Hence the "finds" were gazed at, and wondered at, and then thrown away, perhaps into the sea near which the broch stood. The stones used in the construction of this castle were of large size, and had to be broken up before they could be removed. The original builders must have been possessed both of physical power and mechanical contrivances.

"The Broch of Ness is a very much smaller building at the head of a bay facing the opening in the Firth. A part of the wall is still standing. I do not think it has ever been excavated.

"The broch at the end of Stourbro' Hill has been a large building, but some of the stones lying about appear as if hewn, leading to the supposition that a house had been built in later times out of the ruins but there is, however, no tradition of any such building.

"The ruins in the Holm of Burgawater east of Stourbro' were torn up by Mr Sands some years ago, with what result I do not know. It seemed a small but very ancient building, and the most conspicuous object in it was a large flat stone, supported by four posts, the whole forming a table or platform structure. On the table the women with the Sybil in their midst sang the Vardloker.

"The Broch of West Burrafirth, built in the head of the voe and connected with the land by a bridge of large stepping-stones over which the sea flows at full tide, was still in fair preservation when I last saw it, several feet of the walls, built of large stones, still standing. I think it has been inhabited by the early Vikings, and has been in its day a place of importance, something like Mousa.

"There was also a broch at Nounsbro', Aithsting, but nothing remains of it except the site.

"At Culswick, Sandsting, there was a large broch similar to that at Easter, all now in a heap of ruins. The district is out of the way, and I am not aware if an examination of it has ever been made. But there is another and much more ancient broch at Seffster, Sandsting,—an underground one, and of a kind existing in several parishes in Shetland. They are

The Picts and their Brochs

often found in level fields, dug deep into the ground. These must have formed the earliest abodes of the Norsemen. They are quite different from the mound dwellings or earth houses.

"The conclusion I have come to is that Shetland was inhabited by three successive and distinct races before the arrival of the Norsemen, and that the last of them, the Finns, built the brochs.

"The popular opinion is that the brochs were built by the Picts, a small people. Such could not have been the case. But the Finns were compelled to leave after the Northmen arrived. Before leaving they dismantled their castles, so that the Northmen could not live in them.

"The mound-dwellers took possession of them, and came in contact with the early Udallers. In time the Finn owners were forgotten, and the mound-dwellers, or *Pechts*, became associated in the public mind with the brochs."

Though I do not agree with all the

opinions expressed by Mr. Jamieson, I have quoted from his communication at considerable length, as his remarks, like all he wrote, are exceedingly vivid and suggestive. As will be seen from the following extract, Mr. Jamieson appears to have held some very extraordinary opinions with regard to the early inhabitants:

"Unless old men and women in several parishes wilfully lied, or were more liable to be deceived than we are, the mound-dwellers existed in Shetland up to the beginning of the present century."

I have not attempted to treat of those brochs which have been described by writers of books on Shetland and in the Procedings of learned Societies. The most notable of these is the Broch of Mousa, around which the romantic interest clings that it on two occasions proved a place of refuge for runaway lovers. However romantic the tall tower on the lonely islet may appear, it could hardly have been considered an altogether satisfactory place to resort to for a honeymoon; but if it afforded little comfort to the refugees, its stout walls were an ample defence against the angry kinsmen who beseiged it. Another broch, in the Loch of Clickimin near Lerwick, with its causeway and massive external defences, is perhaps fully more typical of the usual form of Shetland broch. It is now nearly forty years since it was excavated by the Society of Antiquaries, and though it is under the protection of the Ancient Monuments Act, it has suffered much from youthful depredators and other vandals.

In his introduction to the "Orkneyinga Saga," Dr. Anderson gives the following enumeration of known sites of Shetland brochs:—In Unst, 7; in Whalsay, 3; in Yell, 9; in Fetlar, 4; in Mainland and its outlying islets, 51; in Foula, 1—total, 75. This list, however, cannot be regarded as complete.

Few of the Shetland brochs have been

thoroughly investigated; for that purpose considerable funds would be required and competent supervision. In those that have been opened, beyond information regarding their structure little else has been found, but possibly future investigations will throw some light on the obscurity which still envelopes the builders of the brochs.

PREHISTORIC REMAINS

PREHISTORIC REMAINS

OF the early inhabitants of Shetland the brochs and earth-houses are not the only memorials which have come down to us. The implements they used in peace or war are from time to time unearthed in field or moor, and their rubbish heaps, consisting chiefly of the shells of shellfish, are often seen by our shores. Their burial mounds, round which fanciful legends cluster, are frequently met with; and many tall, moss-grown standing-stones remain, mute yet eloquent witnesses of the mystery of the

Shetland Folk-Lore

past. But of these rude monuments we are left with the poet to ask in vain:

"In what age wast raised? at whose command?
If Pictish, or if Scandinavian hand
Sank deep thy base, and bade thee time withstand?"

From the great number of stone implements found in Shetland, it might be supposed that the Stone Age extended over a very long period in these islands. It is probable, however, that even after metal implements were introduced, they did not come into common use for a long period, and that the primitive stone implements were only very gradually displaced. This, it is quite reasonable to suppose, would have been likely to happen in the case of a remote group of islands where we find, even in the present day when there is frequent communication with the mainland, that the *bismar* is still often employed as a weighing machine, and an old world iron fish-oil lamp (the *kollie*) is still used in out of the way places.

Prehistoric Remains

Though there is no proof that the primitive stone implements were made and used by the early people who raised the brochs and dwelt in the ancient earth-houses, tradition attributes them to the Picts. Most of the implements which have been found are rude in form, but may for all that have been well adapted to the purposes for which they were intended. Many, however, are remarkable for the rare skill with which they have been formed, for the beauty of their outlines and the high finish of their polished surface, indicating that the people who fashioned them were possessed of remarkable mechanical skill and exquisite taste.

Primitive man, when he required the use of tools or war weapons, no doubt at first made use of what he found ready to his hand, and accordingly we find waterworn stones which bear traces of having been so employed. In most cases, however, the implements have been chipped or

Shetland Folk-Lore

polished into the form required. Some of these rude implements are of considerable size and weight. The most common type perhaps, is seen in the flat, oblong implement shown in Fig. 2. It is 20 inches in length and 6 inches wide, and was found at Watsness, Walls. Usually examples of this class are much smaller, and very frequently polished at one or both ends.

FIG. 2.—*Rude Stone Implement.*

They are usually composed of sandstone or clay slate, and present great diversity both as regards form and size. Formerly only the finely polished axes were much noticed, but in recent years, since attention has been directed to these rude archaic implements, in some localities considerable quantities have been found, proving them to have been extensively used in early

Prehistoric Remains

times. It is not easy to conjecture with any certainty to what uses they were put. Occasionally club-like handled implements, such as that represented in Fig. 3, are met

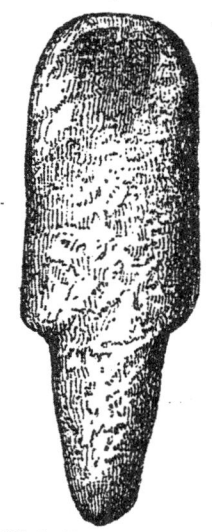

FIG. 3.—*Club-like Handled Implement.*

with. This specimen is of unusually large size, measuring 13½ inches in length by 4 inches wide, and was found in a moss at Burrafirth, Unst. This type of implement is usually made of sandstone with a smooth surface.

These rude stones, evidently shaped by human hands, are found in such numbers that it is evident they must once have been in daily use. Could information be obtained regarding the purposes for which they were employed, it would reveal to us much of the mode of life of the early people at present hidden from us.

It is, however, in the polished celts or axes that the wonderful artistic skill of the Stone Age people is to be seen. In Shetland these finely formed, polished weapons have for ages been looked upon with a kind of superstitious regard, and treasured up from the idea that the possession of one brought luck to the family that possessed it. They were known as *thunderbolts* or *battle-axes*, and were generally believed to have fallen from the sky during a thunderstorm. It used to be thought that to have a battle-axe in a house protected it from being struck by lightning, and it was said

Prehistoric Remains

that, though at other times dry, during a thunderstorm the stone became quite moist.

These weapons are axe or adze shaped and vary considerably as regards size, specimens as small as 4 inches in length and some as large as 14½ inches having been met with. They are frequently composed of serpentine, porphyry, or other hard, finely grained stone suitable for taking a keen edge and high polish. Many of these instruments when found show no traces of having been in use, the cutting edges being as smooth and sharp as when first ground. From the great care evidently displayed in the selection of material and in the finishing of these implements, it is believed that they have been devoted to special use as weapons of war. It is, however, probable that they were also employed as hatchets for hewing wood. When large pieces of timber had to be dealt with, fire was likely used to assist the process, the charred

Shetland Folk-Lore

portions being cut away with these axes. In the peat bogs of Denmark old stems of trees have been found which appear to have been felled in this way, and the American Indians are reported to have hollowed out canoes 30 feet long by means of stone tomahawks, assisted by the use of fire.

When used, the axe was probably fitted into a slot cut through a wooden haft, or into the split end of the wood, and secured by thongs of hide or *term* (cord made from entrails of animals). No traces of any such handles have been found in Shetland, which is not surprising, as the wood was certain to be decomposed lying in the ground. That this, however, is the manner in which these weapons have been used is almost certain from the fact that the stone axes of the South Sea Islanders, which bear an extraordinary resemblance to the weapons of the north, are mounted in this fashion.

It must be remembered that in the early

Prehistoric Remains

times, when the stone implements were in use, trees were growing in the islands, and traces of these ancient woods and thickets survive in the roots which are still found in our peat bogs. That this was the case even after the arrival of the Norsemen seems proved by the appearance of place-names of Norse origin referring to woods and trees. Dr. Jakobsen mentions Skooin Brenda, a place in Quarff, which he derives from Old Norse *skoginn brenda*—the burnt wood; Brennya, a croft in Fladabister, from *brenna*—burnt land; Rees (Quarff), a croft, from *hriss*—brushwood; Krapp, a croft at Gulberwick, from Norwegian *Krape*—brushwood; Hoolin Brenda, a croft at Norwick, Unst, meaning the burnt knoll; and Ribrendadelds, in Setter, North Roe, from *deild*—a portion of land, *brend*—burnt, *ryde*—brushwood. Bruntland, Brunthammarsland, and possibly Lund (Icelandic *Lundr*—a grove) are other examples. The story of the burning of a wood in Foula by the Lewis men

Shetland Folk-Lore

in order to prevent the inhabitants fleeing to it for concealment, is quite in keeping with the customs of the marauding bands of the time, and probably is a tradition of an event which actually occurred. That the Norsemen introduced the art of peat-cutting when wood became scarce is probable, and the bold Jarl Einar likely merited the eke-name he received—Torf Einar. Although the trees growing in Shetland may not have been of very large size, they would have afforded material for agricultural and domestic implements and utensils, for roofs of huts, and for building the frames of coracles or skin boats. The brushwood would also furnish fuel for the inhabitants, and the stone hatchet must have been of as much importance to the Stone Age Shetlander as the *tusker* (spade for cutting peats) is to the crofter of our own day.

The beautiful specimen of a polished axe shown in Fig. 1 (Frontispiece) is from a group of three found lying together in

FIG. 4.—*Stone Axe.*

Shetland Folk-Lore

the soil at Tingwall. They are of porphyritic stone. The largest of the group, Fig. 1, measures 10½ inches in length by 2¾ inches across the cutting face. In the case of the other Tingwall specimen, Fig. 4, which measures 9 inches in length by 3¾ inches, the cutting face is slightly extended, giving it somewhat the appearance of the common form of bronze axe. Possibly this implement belongs to the transition period towards the close of the Stone Age, when it was not unlikely that the forms of the bronze weapons then possessed only by the very wealthy would be imitated in stone as far as that material would permit. Little indication of such an influence, however, is to be seen. On the other hand, it is likely that in the first instance the bronze weapons were modelled on the earlier stone type. The smallest of the three found together at Tingwall is of a less common form. It measures 6½ inches in length by 2 inches in breadth, tapering to about 1¾ inches at the butt,

Prehistoric Remains

which is broader and flatter than usual. One side only is convex, the other, from a

Fig. 5.—*Axe of Porphyrite.*

little above the cutting edge, being slightly hollowed out. This shape was no doubt chosen to make it suitable for being used

Shetland Folk-Lore

as an adze. Though the axe form is probably the most common, distinctly adze-shaped specimens are frequently met with.

Another example of a stone axe, shown in Fig. 5, is thus described by Dr. Anderson in his valuable work, "Scotland in Pagan Times": It "is of greyish porphyritic stone, 10 inches in length, and 3 inches across the centre where it is widest, oval in section, tapering both ways from the middle, upwards to a pointed butt, and downwards to an oval cutting edge. It was found under six feet of peat on the hill above Grimister, called Mount Braa, about two miles from Lerwick."

Another type known as perforated stone battle-axes have occasionally been found. They are hammer shaped, and unlike the ordinary form of stone axes, which were secured in an opening made in the wooden handle, they are pierced with a shaft hole to receive a haft. This variety is, however, rare. Two examples are in the pos-

Prehistoric Remains

session of Mrs. Tulloch, of Leog, Lerwick. The smaller of the two answers closely to the description given by Dr. Anderson, in his "Scotland in Pagan Times," of one found in a barrow in Shetland. It is of a finely mottled stone, beautifully polished, and having a shaft hole ¾ inch in diameter, drilled through the parallel sides. It measures 4½ inches in length, by 1½ inches in width, and in the cross section is a slightly flattened oval. The other axe seems to be composed of finely grained sandstone, and is smoothly finished. It is 5 inches in length, and differs from the smaller specimen in that it tapers slightly from 1½ inches across the face at one end to 1¾ inches at the other. The shaft holes are drilled through the centre of the stone, but nearer one end than the other. These perforated axes also differ from the unperforated, in that the ends are not sharpened. Evidently they were not intended to cut, but they may have been used as war weapons. It is wonderful to think of the patience and skill required by the man who fashioned such a weapon with the imperfect mechanical contrivances at his disposal.

In concluding this brief sketch of the implements belonging to the Stone Age, mention should be made of the stone knives, which are of special interest. Of this class Dr. Anderson remarks: "A series of large, flat, irregularly oval blades of porphyritic stone or madreporite found only in Shetland, have sharper edges, sometimes continued round the whole circumference, sometimes with slightly thickened and blunted backs. They are ground to a smooth, even surface on their flat faces. Another form of knife of which only one complete example exists in the Museum appears also to be peculiar to Shetland—at least, it has not yet been found in any other British locality, though the type is known in the northern parts of Norway. It is a long blade of fissile shale or slaty sandstone, with a more or less

Prehistoric Remains

convex edge, a thickened back, and a projecting tang-like handle. This specimen is 9½ inches in length by 2½ inches across the widest part of the blade. Its surface is ground smooth all over, and the edge is sharpened by grinding from both faces. This variety of implement appears to have been very abundant, though owing to its extreme thinness and consequent fragility it is but seldom that an entire specimen is met with." A fine specimen of the former class of stone knife is in the possession of Mr. Mathewson, Lerwick. It measures 8¾ inches in length by 5½ inches across the broadest part. When it is remembered that these cutting implements were the knives, spokeshaves, and planes of their original owners, it is easy to understand how valuable they were, and with what care they would be fashioned and ground by this early people.

The aborigines made many domestic articles out of *clebber*, or *bairdal*, as steatite is also called. There are stone

Shetland Folk-Lore

lamps which bear some resemblance to the later *kollie, whorls* used as weights for yarn spindles, and perforated stone sinkers for lines. *Knocking stones* and bowls made out of sandstone are found, but most of the smaller vessels that turn up from time to time are of steatite. In several places where the soft soap-stone is found, traces may be seen of the manner in which these vessels were carved out. A good instance of this is to be found in the bed of a burn a little to the south of Vestanore, Cunningsburgh. As the potter's art was practised by the early inhabitants, many of their domestic vessels were made of clay, but owing to the fragile nature of their rude pottery, few specimens of clay dishes have come down to us.

BURIAL MOUNDS.

It would appear that the primitive inhabitants practised cremation as well as earth-burial in the disposing of their dead,

Prehistoric Remains

both customs having the authority of high antiquity. It is not certain that both methods were adopted at the same period, but it is not impossible. Round the graves of this vanished race fancy and curiosity linger, though "when the funeral pyre was out, and the last valediction over, men took a lasting adieu of their interred friends, little expecting the curiosity of future ages should comment upon their ashes; and having no old experience of the duration of their relicks, no opinion of such after considerations." Yet their graves appeal to the popular imagination, and the belief that these *fairy knowes*, as they are called, are the scenes of the nocturnal gambols of the *hillfolk* is widespread. Many of these grass-covered mounds which lie heavy on the forgotten dead are doubtless as old as the brochs, and have been used as places of sepulture by the ancient inhabitants. They are chiefly met with in the neighbourhood of brochs—are low, flattish, circular mounds composed of black-coloured mould mixed with small stones that show the action of fire. Some of these contain in the centre a stone cist. An example of this kind was opened near the burn of Catfirth while cutting for a road. The enclosed cist was formed of four rough flagstones, apparently from a quarry in Bressay. It is very noticeable that they are all found near water, the bank of a burn or the margin of a loch being the common site. The small stones thrown upon the burning heap as offerings for the dead, and copious libations of water from the brook at hand, sometimes formed the rude obsequies at these primitive graves.

There are other ancient mounds of considerable size, perhaps tombs of the great and the wealthy, for—

"Though mean and mighty, rotting
Together, have one dust, yet reverence,
That angel of the world, doth make distinction
Of place 'tween high and low."

So it may be that, under such a great

Prehistoric Remains

mound as that reared at Safester, in "some remote and dateless day" a gallant chief was laid to rest with barbaric dignity and pomp,—

> "Whose gallant deeds
> Haply at many a solemn festival
> The Skald hath sung; but perish'd is the song
> Of praise, as o'er these bleak and barren downs
> The wind that passes and is heard no more."

In some of the large mounds, such as in the Muckle Hjoag, along with considerable quantities of human bones, numbers of cinerary urns have been found, some formed out of stone, others of baked clay. Several large clay specimens have also been discovered in Papa Stour. One of these, which unfortunately is incomplete, a considerable portion of the upper part having been broken away, is made of coarse clay, and exhibits no appearance of decoration. It is $13\frac{1}{2}$ inches in height, but has doubtless been taller when complete. The base is narrow, measuring 5 inches in diameter, and it widens out at the shoulders to a diameter of 13 inches; from the shoulders the lip is curved inwards. It appears to contain ashes, calcined bones, and vitrified stones, indicating the intense heat of the funeral pyre. This urn is in the possession of Mr. James M. Goudie, Lerwick, as is also a large steatite vessel found at Burra, which was probably used as a cinerary urn, as it was said when discovered to have contained ashes. It is square in shape, with slightly sloping sides, and has the corners rounded off; some portions of the top are broken away. It measures 14 inches square and is 5 inches deep, the thickness varying from ¾ inch to 1¼ inches. On the top, as if for a cover, was also found a curious triangular implement of clay slate, the sides measuring about 12 inches and the thickness being about half an inch. Two of the corners are rounded off, and between them an opening has been cut at a slight angle for a hand-grip. The two sides from the point have been chipped to make the edge

Prehistoric Remains

thinner. Along with these a polished celt 11 inches in length was also found.

In the New Statistical Account of Zetland, the Rev. John Bryden, who made an extensive examination of grave mounds in the parish of Sandsting, mentions similar finds: "I have one (an urn) in my possession, which I found under the foundation of the glebe dyke. It measures twelve inches over the mouth, ten inches over the bottom, and is ten inches deep. It contained a quantity of half-burnt bones, and was covered with a pretty heavy stone, flat on the side next to the urn; unfortunately, it was partly broken before I discovered it. There is, however, enough remaining to show its shape and workmanship. I have discovered two other urns on the glebe, filled with a black unctuous earth, but so much decayed that no part of them could be lifted. Out of one of them I removed the earth, and found lying at right angles in the bottom four pieces of broken stone axes."

Shetland Folk-Lore

These rude sepulchral urns suggest nothing of the "flowery tale" which the poet Keats fancied he saw expressed in the Grecian Urn. They speak rather of a state of society rugged and devoid of luxury, where man in sterile, storm-swept isles had too ceaselessly to maintain the mere struggle for existence to devote much attention to Art. They suggest, however, the preparation of the body by weeping women, the solemn procession to the place of burning, the laying of the body upon the tall funeral pile, and the touch of the flaming torch held by the son of the departed, amid the lamentations of sorrowing friends standing around. Then, when the red flames cease to shoot upwards and the body is consumed, careful hands reverently gather the ashes and charred bones into the urn and deposit it in the prepared grave. A flat stone being placed above, the mourners perform the last rite in honour of the dead by heaping up stones to form his cairn, which

Prehistoric Remains

may not be complete at nightfall when men return to the funeral feast.

In a note to the "Corpus Poeticum Boreale," Dr. Vigfusson mentions the interesting circumstance that "Funeral urns of *steatite* (and sometimes of sandstone) are especially characteristic of wicking funerals in the Orkneys, and in those parts of Norway from whence the wickings came and whither they went home to die; they are only met with in Norway *just* at the Wicking Period." It may then have been that their intercourse with the people of the west, including the mainland as well as the isles, may have induced the Vikings to make a change in their funeral customs. As the burial rites of a people are the customs to which they usually most persistently cling, perhaps some other suggestion is needed to account for such a change.

In Shetland the barrows are found upon the hillside and by the seashore, and even beside the refuse heaps of the early inhabitants. Many of them probably belong to a more remote past, but some must have been raised over Vikings who fell in fight, or who, thinking themselves unlucky in this, died a "straw death." When the body was buried uncremated in ancient times, it must have been, in most cases, placed in a bent position with the knees raised up, as the cists are usually from three to four feet in length. The barrows are said to be modelled on the primitive house, and in them the Norsemen believed the dead to dwell. The family tomb was usually near the homestead, and at its side the patriarch sat to learn wisdom from the ancestral spirit buried within.

In the Sagas many stories are told of great and terrible sights witnessed at some of the howes. One of these is found in the Eyrbyggja Saga. It tells of the apparition seen on the death of Thorstein Codbiter, who was drowned about the year 938. He was the son of Rolf, one of the early settlers in Iceland, a great friend of

Thor's and guardian of his temple, for which reason he was called Thorolf, and on account of his magnificent beard (for names had always a meaning in those days), Mostbeard. His son Stein he dedicated to Thor, and called Thorstein. When Thorolf died he was buried in a howe upon Holy Fell, which was a place so sacred that it was not considered fitting that men should even look towards it, and pray with unwashen face. Thorstein one harvest had fared to Hoskuldsey to the fishing, and on an evening while he was away, a shepherd, seeking after his sheep north of Holy Fell, saw the fell open. Inside the fell "he saw mighty fires and heard loud clangour therein and the clank of drinking horns: and when he hearkened, if perchance he might hear any words clear of others, he heard that there was welcomed Thorstein Codbiter and his crew, and he was bidden to sit in the high-seat over against his father." When the shepherd returned, he told what he had witnessed. Next morning men came with the tidings that Thorstein had been drowned at the fishing.

The guardian spirits of the ancient heroes, which in the olden days protected their graves from defilement, in later times have been replaced by the fairies, who should not be angered by the folk contaminating their dwelling places. It is not considered right to drive a stake into one of these mounds, in order to tether an animal; and the same reason has prevented many a howe from being removed, lest the fairies might wreak their revenge by taking the lives of the cattle.

A common belief exists that in these mounds there are hidden "pots of money," and in many cases avarice must have been stronger than superstition, for many of the grave mounds have been already explored. Whatever treasures were discovered were only such as might have enriched the antiquary, but could never repay the searcher after wealth.

Prehistoric Remains

STANDING STONES.

The standing stones, unlike the brochs and the fairy knolls, remain unimpaired by the hand of time, and will stand as mute witnesses of a byegone time for ages yet to come, if let alone by the hand of man. One or more of these may be found in almost every parish of Shetland. They may be seen on the hilltop, as in Burra Isle and in Bressay; or on the sloping hillside, as at Skillister in Nesting, and Clivocast in Unst; and they are also found in low-lying situations, as at Succamires, near Lund. Some of these stones are of great size, and we can only guess by what power, physical or mechanical, they have been transported or erected. The standing stone last mentioned is 12 feet high and measures 24 feet in girth at the base, and will weigh from 20 to 30 tons.

Regarding the purpose of the standing stones we know nothing. They may have been of a commemorative character, erected on the occasion of some remarkable event, as a battle; or they may have been set up to perpetuate the memory of some brave chief. Perhaps they have been raised as witnesses to some covenant between contending or stipulating parties; or lastly, they may have been to the ancient Picts what the Parish Kirk is to the modern inhabitants—a place of worship, where they devoutly assembled under the canopy of heaven to offer their devotions to the Sun-god.

The worship of Baal was perhaps the most widespread of all the ancient beliefs. Its mysteries and bloody rites were observed in the plains of India and on the "high places" of these remote islands. Still a faint memory of it lingers in the fires the children in some places light on midsummer night (Johnsmas), and as of old the priests of Baal danced round their sacred fires, so the boys leap over the flame—thus passing through the fire to Baal. On the other hand, the standing

Prehistoric Remains

stone was a form of memorial familiar both to Celt and to Norseman, and "The Guest's Wisdom," perhaps the earliest of the Eddic poems, contains the lines: "Few roadstones stand by the wayside that were not raised by son to father." In the popular mind they are usually attributed to the giant race, of whom a faint tradition lingers. It was the giant of Roenis Hill who, in his combat with the giant of Papa Stour, threw a stone at his opponent in the distant island, which fell short and is now known as the Standing Stone of Busta. Similar tales are told of other standing stones.

There are no great circles of standing stones in Shetland, such as is found at Brogar, in Orkney. There are, however, circles composed of comparatively small stones. One of the most complete is found in one of the Whalsay Skerries, and is called the "Battle Pund." Doubtless only a modern tradition associates it with the scene of a conflict which Hibbert describes between two parties of fishermen regarding fishing rights. The best known stone circles are those found at Crucifell and Balliasta, Unst, which are preserved in the same condition as in 1774, when they were examined and described by Mr. Low. He gives the dimensions of these circles:

LARGE CIRCLE AT CRUCIFELL.

	Ft.	In.
Diameter of outer stone circle,	55	0
Second or outer earth circle,	45	0
Inner earth circle,	33	6
Nucleus,	10	6

SMALLER CIRCLE.

Diameter of outer circle,	22	0
Diameter of the second,	17	0
Nucleus,	7	6

CIRCLE AT BALLIASTA.

Diameter of the stone circle, little of which now remains,	67	0
First earth circle,	54	9
Second earth circle,	40	0
Nucleus,	12	0

Such places have commonly been held in

Prehistoric Remains

superstitious dread. The person who had the hardihood to walk the Rounds o' Tivla (Crucifell) alone at midnight was proof against fear arising from the presence of *trows*.

Another formation generally consists of three stones. They are commonly called in the districts where they are found *cross stanes*, often pronounced *craw's stanes*. The centre stone is higher than the other two, which form a sort of seat, one at each side of the middle stone. Examples occur, one near the berg of Venstrie, another at Millya Gorda, Unst, and elsewhere throughout the islands.

It may be remarked that the number three enters largely into the superstitions of the Shetlander, as is commonly the case in all mythic lore. For instance, three corbies flying over a house was considered an evil omen, and foreboded a death. Three wishes expressed during the visibility of a shooting star were sure to happen. A fire-brand borne three times round a person or an animal gave them immunity from the influence of *trows*. Three kinds of food offered by three times three mothers was the last and best restorative for a patient that had been rescued from the trolls. The bite of an otter was healed by the application of three hairs from its tail. Live coals falling three times on the hearth was an infallible evidence that statements made at that time were true. These examples may suffice to show how this mystic number is inwrought with our folk-lore.

SCULPTURED STONES.

In addition to the rude obelisks which bear no trace of the workman's chisel, two beautiful examples of sculptured stones have been met with. One of these was found in the ancient churchyard of Collinsburgh, Bressay, and the other discovered in the churchyard of Papil, Burra, in 1877. The latter (Fig. 6) is a slab of finely

FIG. 6.—The Burra Stone.

grained sandstone, 6 feet 10 inches in height, 1 foot 7½ inches wide at the top, and contracting slightly towards the base. The designs are boldly carved, incised lines, except in the case of the four ecclesiastical figures beside the shaft of the cross which stand out in relief. The grotesque animal within the panel in the middle of the stone is said to bear some likeness to the conventional figure of a lion, and probably the resemblance is quite as strong as may be found in many heraldic drawings of the king of beasts. The two semi-human figures at the base are even more strange, the heads having a kind of human look, in spite of the enormous beaks with which they are provided, and the legs which terminate in claws resembling a bird's. Otherwise the figures are evidently intended as human, and each holds an axe which is *not* of the Stone Age type. The beaks of these creatures, it will be noticed, are fixed in a human head placed between them, but from the stone having been

Prehistoric Remains

scaled away it is impossible to determine whether a human figure has been represented or the head only. Though this part of the design is boldly carved and in the same manner as the upper portion, it is not in line with the rest and may have been added by an inferior artist. Though to us it appears grotesque and meaningless, it is possible that it is not a mere example of the ponderous humour of the Stone Age, but that under these quaint forms is concealed some ancient and forgotten myth.

Mr. Gilbert Goudie, Edinburgh, who discovered this interesting relic and had it removed to the National Museum for preservation, considers, no doubt justly, that this monument dates back to early Celtic Christian times. The beautiful form of the cross, as well as the ornamentation, is distinctly of the Celtic type of art, and though there is no inscription upon this monument, yet its resemblance to the Bressay stone, which bears an inscription in Ogam characters, would indicate that it probably belongs to the same period.

The Bressay stone is smaller, being only 3 feet 9 inches in length, 16 inches wide at the top, and tapering to less than a foot at the bottom, but it is richly carved on both sides. It also bears the figure of the cross formed by interlacing lines, and on each side there are two ecclesiastical figures similarly dressed to those on the Burra stone, with long tunics and hoods (*cuculla*), and also holding pastoral staves. These figures have a further resemblance in that two of them are also shown as bearing wallets at their sides, in which probably the Service-Books were carried. The lion-like animal has also its counterpart on the Bressay stone, upon which is also represented, along with some other figures of animals, a man on horseback. Another resemblance is seen in the representation of the figure of a human being between the mouths of two grotesque creatures who appear about to devour it.

Prehistoric Remains

The inscription which is carved on the edge of the Bressay stone has been found difficult of interpretation, as not only are the Ogam characters obscure, but there is uncertainty about the language, which is said to be a mixture of Celtic and Norn. One reading gives for the inscriptions on the edges :

> "The cross of Natdod's daughter here.
> Benres of the sons of the Druid here."

It has been pointed out that Naddod was the name of the Viking who discovered Iceland about 861, and that he had a grandson named Benir. If the Natdod of the Bressay stone is identical with the discoverer of Iceland, the age of the monument would be about a thousand years. It will be remembered that Floki called at Shetland on his voyage to Iceland in 867, and that his daughter Geirhild was drowned in the Loch of Girlsta. It would be a curious coincidence if both the discoverer of Iceland and the man who

Shetland Folk-Lore

followed him and gave the island its name each lost a daughter in Shetland.

Two other stones have also been found in Shetland inscribed with the same Celtic characters. One of these, a large flat slab from Lunnasting, has the inscription on its face; and another, lettered at the edge, was found at St. Ninian's Churchyard, near Bigtown. These are also probably Celtic Christian memorials, but no satisfactory interpretation of the inscriptions has been made, so far as I am aware.

It is very remarkable that while so much has come down to us from the mysterious people who first inhabited the islands, and of whose race and language we know so little, so few traces have survived of the Vikings, who stamped their impression in the place-names of every hill and dale, every rock and skerry, and whose language still forms the main element in the dialect of the islands. While the ruins of the massive towers built by the early people and the weapons

Prehistoric Remains

with which they encountered the Norse invaders in battle still endure, the halls of the sea rovers have disappeared, and the swords and the battle-axes they wielded in many a fierce foray upon the southern coasts are turned to rust.

Perhaps the reason why only a few fragments of runic inscriptions have been found in Shetland is to be found in the fact that the Vikings were too actively engaged in the pursuit of fame and fortune to give much heed to letters, and were content when they sat at home in their high seats to listen to the Skaldic lays and stories of famous fights in far distant lands. Two rune-inscribed stones have been found in Cunningsburgh, but they are incomplete. Another runic inscription is mentioned by Low, who visited the islands in 1774, as having been seen by him at Cross Kirk, Braken, Northmavine, but it has disappeared, as has also the slab which Hibbert stated he found built into the wall of the Church of Sandness. Hibbert, however, was mistaken in describing the stone he found at Sandness as runic, as it was in reality a stone with mirror and crescent symbols carved upon it.

SPEAR HEAD OF BRONZE.

Bronze weapons are reported to have been found in former times, but they have disappeared—either cast aside or given away to visitors from the south, and so as good as lost. That such finds have been made is proved by the following extract from the Diary of a Gentleman specially well informed in all matters relating to the islands. Under date October 1809, he says: "Mr. Arthur Harrison found the following antiquities at Eastness, Northmavine, in digging for a small office-house (*skoe*) he intended to build on a small knoll—(1) a Sword and Dagger; (2) a Stone Hone; (3) a curious instrument, the use of which is unknown [a sketch is given]. All these were lying between

Prehistoric Remains

three flat stones, along with a human thigh bone. He [Mr. Harrison] says the

FIG. 7.—*Spear Head of Bronze.*

Sword and Dagger are neither iron nor steel, but of a similar metal and similarly

Shetland Folk-Lore

blown." The Diarist added that the sword and dagger were unfortunately broken in digging, but that he saw some fragments which he recognised as bronze.

The spear head shown in Fig. 7 is the property of Mr. James W. Cursiter, Kirkwall, who is possessed of a most extensive and valuable collection of Orkney and Shetland antiquities. It "measures $10\tfrac{3}{4}$ inches in length, the socket projecting $3\tfrac{5}{8}$ inches beyond the blade, which is $6\tfrac{3}{8}$ inches in length by $2\tfrac{3}{4}$ inches in extreme breadth. The blade is strengthened by two ribs nearly parallel to the edge. On each side of the socket is a loop of peculiar character, flat, and formed of a lozenge-shaped projection 1 inch long and $\tfrac{3}{4}$ of an inch broad." It was found under a depth of about 4 feet of moss, by a man casting peats at the east side of Sweening Voe, Lunnasting. The spear head is specially interesting as proving that weapons of the Bronze Period found their way to

Prehistoric Remains

Shetland, though very few traces of them now remain.

OVAL BROOCHES OF BRONZE.

The brooch, Fig. 8, illustrated here is

FIG. 8.—*Oval Bowl-shaped Brooch of Bronze.*

one of a pair of oval, shell-shaped breast clasps, 4 inches in length and 2½ inches in breadth, found at Clibberswick, Unst. The design consists of six projecting and pierced ornaments, within which are the indications of six studs, to which stones or glass ornaments were probably originally attached. The whole being enclosed by mouldings and rope design. The brooches were probably worn by women, one on each breast, and the trefoil-shaped ornament (Fig. 9) shown below may have been used as a clasp. They probably belong to the close of the ninth century.

FIG. 9.—*Trefoil-shaped Brooch of Bronze.*

FOLK-LORE

FOLK-LORE

EARLY in the present century many superstitious beliefs and observances were common in Shetland which are now altogether forgotten, or only to be found lingering in some outlying districts. The old world ways of the Shetlanders have given place to a new order of things. Our domestic, social, and industrial life is conducted on different lines. Hence it is evident that even the remembrance of the times of our forefathers will pass away for ever with the present generation. It is hoped that this humble attempt to embalm on the

Shetland Folk-Lore

printed page these recollections of the past will meet with the approbation of every lover of the "Old Rock."

Of all classes, fishermen appear to have been most superstitious. No doubt this arose in a great measure from the nature of their hazardous and precarious calling. The ever fitful wind and changing sea, the lottery of fish catching, the imminent peril and hairbreadth escapes to which they were exposed, fostered a belief in the supernatural.

When a fisherman left his house to proceed to his boat, it was considered most unlucky to call after him, even though he had left something very essential behind; and he was very particular as to meeting a person by the way, lest they should have an "evil eye" or an "ill fit." It was considered a good omen to meet an imbecile or a person deformed from the birth. These were called "Gude's pör," and were suitable *aamas bairns*. After meeting one of such, if the voyage had been at all pros-

Folk-Lore

perous, they were rewarded with an *aamas* or *kjoab*. The person who attempted to cross a fisherman's path when on his way to the boat, intended to do him scathe.

When such was really done, the fisherman, on coming to the point of crossing, took out his *skön* or *tullie* (sea knife), and made a scratch on the ground in the form of a cross, uttering (together with a spittle) the word *twee-te-see-dee*. The sign of the cross was considered an antidote against the intended evil, and the spittle an emphatic expression of contempt for the unchancy hag.

When a crew assembled at their boat at the beginning of the season, each man had his "ain lug o' da taft," or seat for pulling, and this order was never altered. If one had occasion to pass from one part of the boat to another, it was considered very unlucky to go between a man and his *kabe*. On leaving the land the boat was always turned with the sun—from east to west— never in the opposite direction, which was termed *widdershins*. The movements of witches were always made against the sun, and by whirling a wooden *cap* in water or a hand-mill on a bare *looder* (wooden bench on which the mill rested), they were supposed to be able to raise the wind like Furies, and toss the sea in wild commotion capable of destroying anything afloat, from a cock boat to an armada. But to return to the fishermen. Their chief subject of conversation was the weather forecasts. The older and more experienced men would read the sky and explain the various appearances, and there is little doubt that from keen observation they were able to foretell the weather with considerable accuracy. They possessed a stock of weather lore of which we, in these days of barometers and storm-signals, know little.

The movements and conduct of certain birds and animals were looked upon as prognostics of the weather. For example, to hear crows crying after sunset foretold

Folk-Lore

the coming day to be fair. The flight of the rain goose (the red-throated diver) was particularly noticed. When this bird was seen flying in an inland direction the weather was likely to be favourable, but when its flight was directed towards the sea the opposite was expected. Hence—

> "If the rain göse flees ta da hill,
> Ye can geng ta da haf whin ye will;
> Bit whin shö gengs ta da sea,
> Ye maun draw up yir boats an flee."

Cocks crowing or the hens stirring abroad while rain is falling is a sign that it will soon be fair. Flocks of *snaa fowl* (snow bunting) seen before Winter Sunday (the last Sunday of October) foretell the approach of a severe winter.

A cat sitting with her back to the fire indicated cold weather, and washing her face with both the fore paws was a sure prognostic of coming rain; but when puss was observed sleeping on her *harns* (head turned down), fair weather might be expected.

Shetland Folk-Lore

When animals were observed rubbing themselves against stones or fences rain was supposed to be near, and the sensation that caused this behaviour in animals appears to have been felt in the human. An old fisherman might have been heard remarking : " Boys, he's gaein' ta be weet, for dey wir an oondömious yuk i' my head i' da moarnin'." A feeling of langour or tendency to sleep indicated the approach of thunder and rain—hence the saying : " It's fey folk that thunder waukens."

The various articles of furniture about a fisherman's house in the olden days were made from *raaga trees* (drift wood), and certain cracking sounds occasionally heard in such articles were considered sure indications of a change of weather. Sparks flying more than usual from a peat fire foretold the approach of frost ; and if *spunks* (sparks) were seen adhering to the bottom of the *maet* kettle when taken off the fire, snow was near if in winter, and cold, windy weather if in summer.

Folk-Lore

These terrestrial tokens were only secondary. The signs in the heavens above were the special study of the old *hafman*. On these he directed his anxious gaze as he plied the toilsome oar or hauled the fishing line. Halos round the sun or moon (called sun or moon *brochs*) were unwelcome sights, and were anxiously watched to see whether the sun did not "shine them out." It was observed that—

> "When the sun sets in a broch,
> He'll rise in a slauch;
> But if the broch dees awa
> E'er he sets i' da sea,
> He'll rise i' da moarnin'
> Wi' a clear e'e."

That is, if the halo disappears before sunset, the sun is likely to rise in a clear sky, and the following day will be fair. *Brynics* (what appears to be the end of a rainbow) seen on the horizon forbodes squally weather. Large masses of white clouds, called in winter *snaaie heads* and

Shetland Folk-Lore

in summer *eestik heads*, were looked upon with ill favour, as they were sure either "ta rain aff or blaw aff." The *merry dancers* (aurora) extending to the zenith and unusually quick in their movements were considered an ill omen, but when they quietly displayed themselves in a graceful arch along the northern horizon the fishermen expected fair weather. The "carry" or motion of the clouds, with relation to the direction of the wind, was of special interest.

There was a notion that certain days of the week had to do with the weather. For example, a change for the better on Sunday was considered a favourable omen, but a bright Monday betokened a dark week. Wednesday's weather was true, and Friday was supposed to be either the best or the worst day in all the week.

There were certain times of the season when storms were specially expected. These were called *Rees*. There was *Buggle Ree*, about the 17th of March

Folk-Lore

(O.S.); *Paece Ree*, about Easter; *Beltin Ree*, 20th May; and the last three days of March, called the *Borrowing Days*, were generally expected to be boisterous. Most of these weather forecasts may be explained on natural and scientific grounds, but it is not the object of this work to do so.

I shall just mention one other means of foretelling the weather, which doubtless belongs to the Dark Ages of these islands. It is called the *milt token*, and is said to have been practised in some parts of Shetland. When the first *mert* was killed about Hallowmas, the milt or spleen of the animal was taken out and laid on a board, and six cuts were made crosswise, equidistant from each other. These cuts were not quite through the milt, the under side being left whole. They were named—the first, November; the second, December; the third, January; and so on to April. The milt was now laid in a dark place for three days and three nights. It was then carefully examined, and if a cut had closed

Shetland Folk-Lore

and presented a dry appearance, the month it represented was to be mild and dry; but if the cut was open and dry the month was supposed to be windy. An open and wet cut foretold wind and rain.

The Shetland fishermen had quite a vocabulary of old Norse words, which were generally used at sea, particularly when speaking of land objects; and it was deemed most unlucky to neglect the use of these expressions. No doubt the belief lingered that the ancient gods of the Norsemen still exercised power over the mysteries of the *jube* (the depths of the ocean), although their influence was waning before the light of the "White Christ." Hence it was considered prudent to use at least such words as had reference to the old faith. The following names were applicable to wind, etc., in its various degrees:

Gro or *Stö*—Wind in general.
Ungastö—Contrary wind.
Daggastö—Wet wind.
Guzzel—A dry, parching wind.

Folk-Lore

Pirr—Light airs in patches.
Laar—Light airs more diffused.
Stoor—A breeze.
Gooster—A strong breeze.
Gyndagooster—A storm.
Flan or *Tud*—A sudden squall.
Dachin—A lull.
Hain—To cease raining.
Runk—A break between showers.
Röd—Small rain.
Dagg—Wet fog.

The sea, like the wind, in its ever restless moods had various names applied to its movements. *Da mother di* was the name given to the undulations that roll landward even in calm weather, and by means of which the old *hafmen* could find his way in the thickest fog without the aid of a compass.

Di—A wave.
Söal—Swell occasioned by a breeze.
Töve—A short, cross, heavy sea.
Hak—Broken water.
Burrik—A sharp sea or "tide lump."
Bod—A heavy wave breaking on the shore.
Brim—Sound of sea breaking on the shore, especially when land could not be seen, as in a fog.

Shetland Folk-Lore

Brim-fooster—Sea breaking on a sunken rock or *baa*.
Faxin—A *baa* threatening to break.
Overskud or *Ootrug*—Broken or spent water or backwash.
Gruttik—Ebb tide.
Grimster—Ebb during spring tide.
Draag—The drift of a current.
Sokin or *Saagin*—Short period of still water between tides.
Snaar—A turn or whirl in a current.
Roost—A rapid, flowing current, such as Sumburgh Roost and Bluemull Roost.
Haf—The outer fishing ground.
Klak—Inshore fishing ground.
Skurr or *Klakaskurr*—Inshore fishing seat.
Fram—To seaward.

There were several names applied to the sea bottom, such as the *flör*, the *maar*, the *jube*, the *graef*, and the *ljoag*.

The old fishermen never spoke of things being lost or broken, and they never mentioned the *end* of anything. To be lost was expressed as having "gone to itself"; broken, "made up"; and the end was called the *damp*.

These were the chief terms applied to wind and sea, but of course they varied

Folk-Lore

somewhat in different localities. The boat also, and its furniture, together with land, animals, and other objects, were distinguished in the same quaint nomenclature, e.g.:

Faar—Boat.
Rae—Yard.
Stong—Mast.
Skegg—Sail.
Raemiks—Oars.
Bigg or *Bö*—House.
Frö or *Da Haimelt*—Wife.
Upstaander or *Baeniman*—Minister.
Yarmer or *Loader*—Precentor.
Fjandin—Devil.
Birtik—Fire.
Groitik—Meat-kettle.
Gludder or *Föger*—Sun.
Gloamer—Moon.
Boorik—Cow.
Nikker, Snegger, or *Soopaltie*—Horse.
Bjaener or *Hokner*—Dog.
Voaler, Vengie, Foodin, or *Krammer*—Cat.
Footik—Mouse.
Dryilla-skövie or *Dratsie*—Otter.
Flukner or *Klaager*—Hen.
Da Fish, Da Glyed Shield, or *Baldin*—Turbot.
Fjaedin—Whale.

Shetland Folk-Lore

Much valuable information regarding the significance and derivation of these and other old words used in Shetland may be found in Jakobsen's "Shetland Dialect and Place-Names."

The whale or *fjaedin*, or *bregdie* (as some of these aquatic monsters were called), was very much dreaded by the old fishermen, especially when one was seen alone. But they had means for protecting themselves against these dark denizens of the deep. This was simply an old copper coin. As soon as a whale was seen in close proximity to a boat, the copper penny was held in the water and scraped with a steel knife. It was believed that no whale would approach a boat so protected, and the fishermen soon had the pleasure of seeing their uncanny visitor give them a wide berth.

It was generally believed that steel instruments and silver coins possessed wonderful virtue in counteracting the malevolence of witches and *trows*. To

Folk-Lore

cross witches above the breath, *i.e.*, on the forehead, so as to draw their *drörie* (blood) with a steel *noraleg* (a needle with the eye broken), deprived them of their power to hurt. A steel knife stuck in the mast of a boat was used as a means of raising the wind; but some old fishermen would rather have rowed in a calm than had recourse to this expedient, which it was said had been the overthrow of some.

A story is told in verse by one of the Scotts of Lund of a belated traveller who was sorely pressed by a swarm of *hillfolk* or *trows* near the Heugins o' Watley:

"Whin Johnnie cam' ta Watley burn,
They (*trows*) tried to dö 'im an ill turn;
Bit haein his gun weel lod,
He cocked an' fired ta clear da rodd.
Bit Johnnie's gun refused ta fire,
Which made 'im cry: "O, dems er dier";
Then in the barrel he did drive
English shillings number five,
Which into bodies did divide
That walked close by Johnnie's side."

When instruments of domestic use or

weapons of warfare made of iron took the place of the old stone implements, their wonderful powers and superiority over the latter were no doubt attributed to magic. Hence the peculiar virtue of steel may be accounted for; and the proverbial expression "as true as steel," when speaking of anything that is reliable or trustworthy. When an animal or even a person had died suddenly, they were supposed to be *elf-shot*; and it was said that the elfin arrow was sometimes found: a minute, three-sided dagger of the finest steel.

THE HAF FISHING.

The old Shetland *sixern* or *haf* boat is now becoming obsolete. The great storm of 1881 appears to have given the death-blow to this time-honoured craft and to the old mode of fishing. The model is still preserved in the build of small boats, which in proportion to their size are the safest craft afloat.

Folk-Lore

About the beginning of the century they were modelled in Norway and temporarily put together there with *timmer pins*. The pieces were numbered and shipped in

FIG. 10.—*Shetland Sixern.*

bundles to Shetland, where local carpenters were employed to "set them up," or put the parts together with *seam and röv*, and make them ready for sea. In selecting a new boat, the service of an expert was commonly required to examine the *börds*, in order to detect the presence of *windy knots* or *wattery swirls* in the wood. The presence of these indicated that the boat was liable to *störa-brooken*, *i.e.*, blown up by the wind on land, or *misförn* at sea.

I was told by an old man that he called on a brother-fisherman to examine a boat that he had got built. After a careful overhaul of the newly built craft, he said : " Doo may hae a heavy haand, bit never a faerd haert. Watter 'ill no hurt dy boat, bit wind will. Tak' my wird, an' shord 'er weel." For ten long years this boat was used with safety and success, and every time she returned from sea was *yerd-fasted* in the winter *noost*. It came to pass, however, on a fair September night that they landed from the *piltik eela*, intending to make an early start for the ling *raiths*. As there were no signs of an impending storm, the boat was temporarily shored on

Folk-Lore

the beach; but before morning a sudden squall from the west had tossed the doomed craft to pieces among the rocks.

The old *haf* boat measured from 18 to 20 feet of keel, the stems bending outwards in a graceful curve, so as to give a length of some 26 feet over all. The breadth of beam was 6 to 7 feet, and the depth of hold 27 inches. The boat was divided into six compartments, viz., *forehead, fore-room, mid-room, oost-room, shott, hurrik* or *kannie*. This last compartment next the stern was occupied by the steersman. The *shott* was double the size of a *room*, and formed a sort of hold in which the fish was carried. The various *rooms* were separated from each other by *fiska brods* (fish boards); and, in ordinary circumstances, a well-equipped boat had a place for everything and everything in its place. The sail, when not in use, was stowed in the fore-head, together with the buoys, buoy-ropes, and handline reels. The bread-box and *blaand* keg occupied the fore-room, while the ballast was placed in the mid-room, where the mast stood. The oost-room was always kept empty for the purpose—as its name implies—of *ousing* or discharging water.

Each man's share of *tows* or lines was termed a *packie*, and consisted of from 12 to 16 *bouchts* or hanks of lines, each measuring 40 fathoms. The hooks of wrought iron were *wupped* to *bidds* about four feet long, and placed along the ground line at a distance of nine yards apart. The fleet of lines carried was thus very considerable—extending to over four miles, and mounting 900 to 1000 hooks.

With reference to fishing hooks, it may be mentioned here that prior to the introduction of iron or steel hooks fish were caught by means of a small bit of hard wood or a splinter of bone from two to four inches long, attached to the end of the *tome* or *skoag*. This pin with the bait was held in position by a wrapping of coarse wool called *vaav*. When the fisher-

Folk-Lore

men "felt 'im" (became aware of a fish biting), he "gi'ed 'im da fadam," *i.e.*, he hauled in an arm's length of line with a sudden jerk. The *vaaving* that held the *vaarnakle* or *berjoggel* (the wooden hook or rather pin) in an upright position now relaxed, and it turned horizontally across the mouth or throat of the fish, holding it fast while the fisherman gently drew it to the boat amidst profound silence, as it was deemed most unlucky to speak while a fish was being hauled. Long after the introduction of the modern hook, fishermen still used *vaav* when fishing with very soft bait. Formerly sinkers were made of *klamal* or soap-stone, instead of lead as at present, and to this day fishermen speak of the *haandline stane* or *lead stane*, a remnant of the ancient practice. Quite recently one of these ancient sinker stones was lifted on a fish hook at a *haf seat* off the north part of Unst.

These frail boats ventured a good distance from the land. Rönies or Rönis

Hill (as Dr. Jakobsen prefers to spell it) in *skut*, or the Pobies *dippin'*, was by no means among the "crabs and *drooielines*," but signified a distance of thirty miles from the shore.

The fishermen were very particular to set their lines in a given straight course, indicated by *meiths* or marks on the land. This was chiefly to enable them the more readily to find the lines in the event of *making up* (breaking), and it was further considered that certain kinds of bottom kept fish more readily than others, and these patches of ground were known by names, sometimes that of the discoverer, as Maan's Raith, Tammas' Grund, Tirvil's Seat, etc.; but frequently they were distinguished by names having reference to their landmarks, as the Heug an' da Rimble, the Nippin Grund, the Vords, Hagmark an' da Röcok, etc. The fishing grounds nearest the land were called *klaks*, where handline fishing was practised, and were marked by cross *meiths*, so as to find

Folk-Lore

the exact spot. These were called *klakaskurrs*, and sometimes *seats*, and were named chiefly from their landmarks. Perhaps in some cases their names were indicative of the kind of bottom, as quite a number of these names ended in the suffix Mö, as Hoolnamö, Helyersmö, Fjelsmö, Tongamö, etc. Now, all these have soft or sandy bottoms, which may be implied in the particle Mö.

Outside the inshore fishing grounds, some five or six miles from land, were the *fram seats* or *raiths*, all marked and named as I have described. The usual fishing practised here was by handline, but the *haf* lines were also set during *aevaliss* (unsettled) weather.

Let us, gentle reader, imagine ourselves on board a *haf* boat. The crew have just completed the "setting" of the *tows*. The *bow* (buoy) is floating close at hand, attached to the boat by means of a *vaar-line*. Not a breath stirs the air, not a wave disturbs the bosom of the deep.

Shetland Folk-Lore

The ocean mirror reflects the many-tinted cloudlets sprinkled o'er the vault of heaven. The sun has set to us, and his golden rays have ceased to dance o'er the ripples; but Pobies' brow, still bathed in a flood of crimson light, sphinx-like rising from the waters, peers *framwards* like a sentinel of Night. No human being is in sight; a lazy-looking gull alone bears us company. Six weary hours of toil have passed since the crew had their last meal, and now they prepare to take supper. The skipper opens the *buggie* (a bag made of sheepskin), and takes out three *biddies* (very thick oatcakes), each of which he cuts in halves with his *sköne* (sea-knife). Handing a piece to each man, he expresses himself very reverently in the following terms: "Gude hadd Dy haand ower wis. Open da mooth o' da mamik (a ling having a roe), an' bring wis safe ta da kaavies (land)." Here was a prayer to God for preservation, guidance, and success, in a few syllables, more compre-

Folk-Lore

hensive and sincere than that uttered by the learned *upstaander* (minister). This humble meal of dry bread is washed down with a drink of *blaand* (a kind of whey made from buttermilk), after which the snuff-horn is passed round, and every man takes a pinch. It is noticeable that the crew in their conversation seldom give a negative reply. Instead of their saying " No," we hear *by-ye-blithe*.

It is now the *swaar o' dim* (midnight), and time to haul the *tows*. The east tide has *saaged* (ceased to flow), and the lines have got the *wast turnin'*. The distant hilltops are no longer visible. A thin veil of *ask* (haze) hangs o'er the horizon. We are now alone on the wide waste of waters. The gull that kept us company has gone to roost in the distant *maa-craig*. Nothing living can be seen save the occasional glint of a petrel footing the ripples.

Two of the crew, preparing to haul (or *hail*, as it is commonly pronounced), dress themselves in their leather *jubs* and *barm* skins. The man who hauls stands in the *oost-room*, face to *linebörd* (starboard); the other man sits astride the *shott* thwart. His work is to take in the fish, unhook and deposit them in the *shott*. His *sköne*, *huggie-staff* (fish-clip), and *kavel-tree* are at hand. He peers intently into the water as the line is being hauled. At length his hand seizes the *huggie-staff*, and knocking on the gunwale, he utters the word "Twee" (drawing the *ee* very long). This is no sooner said than he calls out "Wheeda"; and presently he exclaims: "Wheeda-hint-da-wheeda!" What does all this mean? It is glad tidings. The short prayer at supper-time has been answered—"da mooth o' da mamik" has been opened. It means that three ling are being hauled up hook after hook, and that the whole three are visible through the clear water to the eye of him that holds the *huggie-staff*.

Presently a smile of pleasure may be seen on the face of the man that hauls the line. He feels a heavy weight and knows it to be the *nud o' a fish* (*i.e.*, a halibut, which is never named, but always spoken of as *da fish* or *da glyed shield*). Nothing comes more welcome to the gunwale of the *haf* boat. It provided a valuable *nabert* (bait), and on its toothsome fish the crew feasted when on shore. The *blugga-banes* of the halibut were stuck in the *wáa o' da lodge* and under the *eft hinnie spot o' da sixern* for luck. A large skate frequently formed part of the catch, and when deposited in the *shott* its formidable caudle appendage was a source of annoyance to the man in the *kavel*, until he took his *sköne* and *sneed aff her skövie* (cut off the tail). The hauling of the lines in ordinary circumstances occupied from four to six hours.

It will be readily understood that these small boats, going to such a distance from the land and having such a length of lines to haul by hand, would be frequently overtaken by a storm, and ran the risk of being overwhelmed in making the wild headlands of Shetland. Though accidents did occur, yet it is matter for surprise that they were not more frequent. This was not so much owing to the sea-worthiness of the boats themselves, as to the skill and dexterity with which they were handled, In old times they never used the sail except they could "lie course." When a storm came off the land they manned the oars and *andowed* ahead; and if the storm continued any length of time with severity, they ran the risk of being driven off and lost. But the most dangerous sailing, and that which required the most dexterous management, was running before the wind in a storm.

We shall again imagine ourselves on board a *haf* boat. The wind is blowing towards the land in angry gusts. The billows of the heavy ground swell toss their heads on high, and burst in angry roar. The waves chase each other in wild confusion. How frail does our craft

Folk-Lore

appear! tossed like a chip midst the ceaseless heave. The old skipper ships the rudder. God bless his weather-beaten face and nerve his hand to hold the helm. All he can do is to steer a straight course. Billows to right of him, billows to left of him, billows behind him, threaten to whelm him. But another also has a charge, and on him mainly does our safety depend. This is the man who holds the halyards (the *towman*), and has control of the sail.

When everything is ready the sail is hoisted, and the *towman* grasps the halyards. In one hand he holds the hoisting part and in the other the downhaul. Like a frightened steed the boat runs before the gale. Presently an angry wave comes rolling in our wake, and as it overtakes us we appear to be plunging headlong into the abyss of the waters; but the man who holds the halyards instantly lowers the sail a few feet so as to retard our motion. We seem for the moment to be hanging on a pivot of unstable water, but the wave

Shetland Folk-Lore

passes on ahead and the sail is hoisted so as to accelerate our speed, and following close on the back of the spent sea, we run away from the succeeding wave. Meanwhile fish liver is being crushed in the *oost-room* and thrown on the troubled waters.

Sailing in a heavy sea, with the wind on the beam, the steersman has full control. He holds helm and sheet. This is also dangerous sailing, and requires expert management. The state of the sea along our path, both ahead and to windward, is carefully watched, and the boat is zigzagged so that, if possible, breaking seas may be shunned; but it often happens that an angry "lump" will toss itself in close proximity to our frail craft, so near that it may break aboard. But the man at the helm measures the wave with his eye, and if it threatens to strike the boat before the mast, the helm is put down and the sheet run off. The boat's head is thus brought towards the wave, which it vaults with the

Folk-Lore

agility of a stag. But on the other hand, if the wave is likely to strike abaft the mast, the helm is put up with all speed, and the boat flees away from the angry wave, leaving it to spend its fury astern.

TROWS AND WITCHES.

About the middle of May the wives set their *kirns*, *milk-spans*, and *raemikles* (butter kits) in the *well stripe* to steep. The youngsters were employed to search for four-leaved *smora* (clover), the finding of which was considered extremely lucky, and anyone possessed of this holy plant was considered proof against the evil designs of witches.

Johnsmas was the season when witchcraft was most dreaded, and persons skilled in the black art deprived their neighbours of the profit of their milk and butter. Every housewife tried to keep her own, and used every precaution which seemed to her essential for this end.

Shetland Folk-Lore

Persons intent on witching a neighbour endeavoured to obtain the loan of some domestic utensil, especially about the time when a cow was expected to calve. But a wise woman would lend nothing at such a time. If a suspected person called, and even asked for a "drink o' *blaand*," the guidwife would seize a *lowin taand* (live coal), and chase the uncanny visitor out the door, throwing the fire after her, while she exclaimed: "Twee-tee-see-dee, du ill-vaum'd trooker!"

But it was difficult to preserve one's self from scathe, as the profit was supposed to be taken by such simple means as stepping over a cow's tether, plucking a handful of grass off the byre wall, or crossing a woman's path when on her way to milk the cows. Hence, in spite of every effort to prevent them, it often happened that witches carried out their dark designs at the expense of an artless neighbour.

When a person had good reason to believe that their cows had been witched,

Folk-Lore

they commonly adopted such means as were considered most effectual in detecting the witch and bringing back the lost profit. This was sometimes a most elaborate affair, and required a considerable amount of nerve for its performance.

The following was related to me many years ago as having been done. A woman who suspected that her cows had been witched repaired to a march between two lairds' lands, and pulled fifteen green nettles by the roots. These were bound in a sheaf and placed on the *looder* of a water-mill.

Then the woman, providing herself with a triangular clipping of *skrootie claith*, two *noralegs*, a flint and steel, and a box of tinder, went to the mill at the hour of midnight, and taking the bundle of nettles, wended her way to the kirkyard of the parish. Arriving there, she went to the east side of the yard, and crossed the dyke back foremost.

Shetland Folk-Lore

Selecting an open space, the nettles are unloosed, and twelve of the number are placed end to end so as to form a circle. They are counted out backwards, while the following formula is slowly repeated:

" Da twal, da twal Apostles ;
Da 'leven, da 'leven Evangelists ;
Da ten, da ten Commandments ;
Da nine, da brazen shiners ;
Da eight, da holy waters ;
Da seven, da stars o' heaven ;
Da six, Creation's dawnin' ;
Da five, da timblers o' da bools ;
Da four, da gospel makers ;
Da tree, da triddle treevers ;
Da twa lily white boys that clothe themselves in green ;
Da een, da een dat walks alon', an' evermore sall rue."

Two of the remaining three nettles are now placed in the centre of the circle in the form of a St. Andrew's Cross. The two *noralegs* are also stuck into the *claith* in the form of a cross. Then with the *noralegs* in the one hand and the odd nettle in the other, she takes

Folk-Lore

her stand within the sacred circle and exclaims:

> "With this green nettle
> And cross of metal
> I witches and wierds defy;
> O' warld's gear gi'e me nae mair
> Than the luck back ta da kye.
> Whae'er it be, else he or she,
> Dat's hurtit me an' mine,
> In sorrow may dey live an' dee,
> In pörta may dey pine."

Then, suiting the action to the word, she sets fire to the tinder, saying: "So perish all my foes."

This wierd performance is now over, the nettles are collected, and the woman returns to her home in the small hours of the morning. The nettles are buried in the *gulgraave o' da vyeadie* (open drain) of the byre. The *noralegs* are stuck into the byre wall near the *vagil baand* of the cow, and as both rotted and corroded, so the witch was supposed to be seized with some wasting disease.

Trows or *hillfolk* were supposed to be

Shetland Folk-Lore

possessed of like passions as we are. They married and were given in marriage. They indulged their appetites in the good things of this life even as we do. They even required the services of the children of men for fiddlers, *howdies*, *gulyas*, and nurses, and there are alive to this day persons whose forebears were said to be so employed.

They, however, were not always friendly with men. They sometimes set covetous eyes on sheep and cattle, and on women and children. When they wished to take a nice *mert* (fat cow), they did not remove the animal to their own subterranean abodes, leaving no trace above ground; but the cow, to all appearance, was still in the possession of its owner, pining away under some unknown disease, and was said to be "elf-shot."

A crofter in a certain parish had a cow supposed to be "hurt frae da grund," and an old woman called Maron o' Nort'-a-Voe —a famous witch doctor—was sent for.

Folk-Lore

On arriving at the house, Maron sent the goodman to the seashore to procure three crabs, of a kind called *cra's lupiks*. Meanwhile Maron provided herself with a *puttik* of tar, a steel *noraleg*, a leaf from a Bible, and a *lowin taand.* Thus equipped, she enters the byre. The cow is resting on the *bizzie*, unable to rise or eat.

Waving the fire-brand, she marches round the cow three times, against the sun, giving the beast a severe stab at each turn with the needle. The poor animal now jumps to its feet, while Maron proceeds to wave the leaf of holy writ over its back, at the same time muttering certain inaudible words in Norse. The fire-brand is placed in the tar pot and set at the cow's head, the smoke or *sneuker* of which excites a fit of coughing on the trembling animal. A cat is now brought on the scene, and set on the cow's neck, and dragged by the tail three times over the cow's back. Presently the old man arrives with the fairy crabs, and these are given in one dose all alive and kicking. Maron has now done her duty; the cow is delivered from the power of the *trows*. She leaves instructions that the ashes of the *taand* and the tar that remain in the pot be made into three pills, and these are to be given to the cow *blöd fastin* on three mornings.

The writer can remember a woman who claimed to have been taken by the *trows*, but who was mercifully delivered from their power by the skill of a famous witch-doctor.

It happened in this wise. When the woman, whose name was Meg, was nine months old, her mother left the child asleep in the cradle, and went into the byre to milk a cow. While thus engaged, she heard the child utter a terrible scream, and rushing into the house she found the bairn struggling and crying in a most excited manner. In vain she tried to soothe the child, in vain she sang sweet lullaby. Poor Meg cries and will not be comforted. She gets blue in the face and

Folk-Lore

hoarse in the throat, and altogether so changed that even the mother cannot recognise her once thriving child. At last an old woman is brought to the house, and she declares that the bairn is "hurted frae da grund."

A bucket of salt water is fetched out of the breaking sea, and three small *ebb-stanes*. A large fire is put on the hearth and the stones are placed in it. The sea water is poured into the meat kettle, and the stones when red hot are thrown into it. Meg is stripped and placed in this bath. She is turned round in the kettle, three times with the sun and thrice in the opposite direction.

The child is now placed on a wet blanket, and passed through the flame of the peat fire three times. She is then swathed in this sheet and put to bed, after which she is burned in effigy. The mother is further instructed to "tig the nine mothers' maet" for the bairn's restoration—*i.e.*, nine mothers whose first born were sons are each solicited for an offering of three articles of food, to be used during the convalescence of the patient who has been thus snatched from the power of the *trows*. Meg lived to a good old age, and often related the story of her recovery to the writer.

The Wart o' Cleat in Whalsay was inhabited by *trows*, and many fair damsels were lured to this fairy abode, where they lived and brought forth children, who were changed into a sort of semi-spiritual existence. Consequently the service of skilled women of the daughters of men was in frequent demand.

Once it happened that the *trows* of Cleat sent a messenger to the mainland to fetch a *howdie* who dwelt in Lunna Ness; but the woman delayed to cross the Sound owing to the raging of the sea. At last, however, she consented to follow her guide, and setting out, bearing two kits of *faavers* (dainty meats) for the patient, they reached the eastern side of

Folk-Lore

the Ness. Here they were met by another messenger from trowland, come to hasten their journey; but when the woman caught sight of the angry sea, she stood hesitating to cross. This conduct so exasperated the *trows* that they transformed her and the two kits into stone. The three stones stand there to this day as a warning to others who should hesitate to obey the *trows*.

Now, from the following legend it would appear that such fears were unnecessary. There lived in Fraam Gord a woman called Catherine Tammasdaughter, who practised midwifery. One dark, stormy night, as she and her husband were asleep, a messenger from the *trows* appeared at the bedside. Instead of the goodman getting up and having a say in the matter, he is thrown by a magic spell into the most profound slumber, so that he is quite oblivious to his wife's departure.

Catherine is soon ready, and is conducted to the seashore, where a small boat is in waiting. The night is dark and murky, and the sea is breaking on the shore, but fearlessly she takes her seat in the tiny skiff. With amazing speed they skim the waves, and soon she is landed in the Wick o' Gröten, in the island of Fetlar. Presently she is ushered into a spacious cavern, where a great company of strange beings are gathered together. The special object of Catherine's visit is soon accomplished, and she is presented with a tiny *pig* (jar), containing an ointment for anointing the new-born child. While she is performing this delicate operation, she accidentally touches one of her eyes. No sooner does the mysterious ointment touch the eyelid than she beholds a certain woman of her former acquaintance, who had been some time dead. Calling her by name, she exclaims: "Lass, what w'y is du come here?" "What e'e saw du yon wi'?" enquires one of the *trows*. "Dis ene," replies Catherine, pointing to her left eye. Im-

Folk-Lore

mediately by an *elf-shot* she is struck blind on the eye that had been thus mysteriously opened to behold the secrets of this enchanted dwelling.

It is said that the *trows* were great lovers of music, and the fiddlers of the olden time could discuss lightsome lilts, known as "fairy reels," that had been learned from the *hillfolk*. A noted fiddler named John Herculeson had been invited to a wedding at Whiteness, where he was supposed to arrive early on the bridal e'en. The company waited long and patiently, but John did not turn up, and it was only on the eve of the "sindering day" that he reached the festive dwelling. Now, it turned out that John, while crossing the Hill of Wormidale, had been taken into a *trowie* abode, and had been kept playing the fiddle for two whole days. It was deemed imprudent to accept any reward from the *trows*, or to partake of their food.

I was told by an old man of my early acquaintance that on one occasion he was crossing Valafell in the gloaming of an autumn day, and being weary, he sat down to rest at the foot of Gulla Hammar. Not a breath of wind stirred the air; nor sound was heard, save the murmuring of the gentle waves that laved the adjacent shore. Presently he heard the strains of sweet music vibrating among the crevices of the rocks overhead. So distinct and continuous were the sounds that he learned the piece by ear, and subsequently taught it to a fiddler, who classed it among his best dance music, under the name of "The Trowie Reel."

A few legends of the fabled race of giants have come down to us. These stories are usually connected with the standing stones, or remarkable rocks or boulders.

A story is told of two giants called Herman and Saxe, who once lived in Unst. The former resided in a capacious *helyer* (cave) in the neighbourhood of Hermaness, called Herman's Ha', while

Folk-Lore

Saxe occupied a subterranean cavern in the side of the Muckle Pobie, called Saxe's Ha' to this day. Now, it happened that Herman had captured a whale at Burrafirth, and as it was exceptionally large, he asked neighbour Saxe for the loan of his kettle (a great, cauldron-shaped cavity in the rocks), in which to boil his gigantic prey. But Saxe, having an eye to business, would only lend the kettle on condition that he got half of the whale. These terms seemed exorbitant to Herman, and indignant at the churlish conduct of his neighbour, he seized a huge boulder and hurled it at Saxe. But, unlike the giant of Rönies Hill, he overshot the mark, and the stone fell into the sea near the Horns o' Haggmark, where it stands high above the waves, and bears the name of Herman's Stack.

A standing stone once stood near the old churchyard of Norwick, in Unst, which was also connected with the giant of the kettle. This stone had a hole in it, and its origin was traditionally said to be as follows. The giant Saxe came to Kirkatoon, where dwelt a famous *howdie* (midwife), whose services were required at his residence, and not finding a suitable fastening for the beast that he had brought to carry the *cummer*, he drove the monolith into the ground and pushed his thumb through it, making a hole, into which he tied his horse's rein.

About the beginning of the century doctors were few and far between, and the professional V.S. altogether unknown.

Although our forefathers enjoyed a greater immunity from disease than we, whose constitutions are weakened by a foreign dietry, yet then, as now, both man and beast were liable to disease, the true nature of which was a mystery to our forefathers. In every parish there were persons who claimed to be possessed of the power to treat the sick. Most forms of illness were supposed to be either an "evil onwaar," or "hurted frae da grund." The former was the result of the evil prayer or wish of some wicked person skilled in the black art, the latter was the supernatural influence of *trows* or *hillfolk*. When a person fell sick, some skilful neighbour was at once called in and the person carefully examined.

If there was any tendency to shortness of breathing, the patient was asked to "pick the mills." This was done by repeating the following without drawing breath:

"Four-and-twenty millstanes hang upon a waa,
He was a good picker that picked them aa:

Picked ene,	Picked thirteen,
Picked twa,	Picked fourteen,
Picked tree,	Picked fifteen,
Picked four,	Picked sixteen,
Picked five,	Picked seventeen,
Picked six,	Picked eighteen,
Picked seven,	Picked nineteen,
Picked eight,	Picked twenty,
Picked nine,	Picked twenty-one,
Picked ten,	Picked twenty-two,
Picked 'leven,	Picked twenty-three,
Picked twal,	Picked twenty-four."

If the patient could pick eighteen to

twenty-four mills, the breathing or lungs were supposed to be in a fairly good condition, but if the sufferer further complained of having "lost dir stamack" (appetite), they were supposed to be afflicted with the "heart wear."

This disease assumed two forms, viz., the *aaber* and the *feckless*. In the former the heart was understood to be too big, and there was a voracious (*aaber*—greedy) appetite, without doing the body any good. In the latter—or *feckless* form—the heart was supposed to be wasting away under some *trowie* influence, and there was no desire for food. "Castin' or rinnin' da heart" and "tiggin' da nine women's maet" were the chief applications for these complaints.

The "castin' o' da heart" was performed as follows. A small quantity of lead was melted in a *kollie*, and the patient was set in the meat kettle before the fire. On the head was placed a blind sieve, in the centre of which a bowl of water was set. A pair of steel scissors or two keys were held in the hand of the operator in the form of a cross, and through the *bool* of the scissors or key the molten lead was poured into the water. The numerous shapes assumed by the lead were carefully examined, and the operation was repeated until a piece was found in form like the human heart. This was sewn in the left breast of some article of underclothing and worn by the patient for three moons. Further, the water used in this ceremony was made into porridge, of which the patient partook seated in the "guit o' da door," at the hour of sunset. In casting the heart, attention was paid to the moon: for the *aaber* heart-wear the time chosen was the waning moon and the ebbing tide, and for the *feckless* form the opposite was deemed the most fitting time.

The most serious forms of disease were "mort-caald" and "inbred fever," which no doubt corresponds with our bronchitis and influenza. *Gulsa*, or the yellow

Shetland Folk-Lore

disease (jaundice), was treated by an oil obtained from the *gulsa whelk*, or garden snail.

In sprained joints the *wrestin treed* was considered the best remedy. This thread was made of black wool, and knotted in a peculiar way, viz., a knot for every day in the moon's age. This was tied round the sprained joint, the operator muttering in an undertone:

> "Da Loard raed,
> Da foal slaed,
> Sinnin ta sinnin,
> Bane ta bane,
> Hael i' da Father,
> Da Son, an' da
> Holy Ghost's name."

Burning and toothache were "told out" by uttering over the patient certain formulas of words in Norse, only known to the speaker. Ringworm was "told out" in a rather peculiar way. The practitioner took three straws, on each of which were three knots or joints, and lighting these in the fire, the following words were uttered while the straws burned:

> "Ringwirm, ringwirm, red,
> Saand be dy maet
> An' fire be dy bed;
> Aye may du dwine,
> An' never may du spread."

Then the part affected was dusted over with the ashes of the burned straws, and the unburned parts were deposited under a *mör fael*.

For sprains and bruises, and affections of an inflammatory nature, a form of cupping called *horn blöd* was very frequently employed, and even yet is not quite obsolete; and I am of opinion that no more effectual mode of cupping or local bleeding can be practised.

The *blöd-horn* was commonly made of the horn of a quey or young cow. It was about four inches long, and from an inch and a half to two inches in diameter at the wide end. The horn was scraped and dressed, the small end being perforated

Shetland Folk-Lore

and wrapped round with a bit of dried bladder. The operator sucked the horn to the affected part, thus making a circle on the skin. The spot thus marked was *saxed* or scarified so as to bleed. The horn was now applied, the contained air being extracted by sucking with the mouth. The pressure of the external air caused the folds of the bladder to shut the perforation of the horn, and thus prevented the ingress of air from without. In order to accelerate the flow of blood and reduce the local inflammation, a warm fomentation was applied round the base of the horn. *Howdies* generally possessed *blöd-horns*, and were the chief practitioners.

Recourse was often had to certain waters that were supposed to possess healing virtues. Helga Water, in Northmavine, and Yelabrön or Hielyaburn, in the island of Unst, were famous for their health-giving properties, as the names seem to imply. The latter is one of the finest springs in the island, flowing with

Folk-Lore

undiminished abundance during the most prolonged drought of summer, bubbling up from a gravelly bed as clear as crystal. Regarding this spring the story is told of a certain priest who came to teach the old inhabitants the doctrine of the "White Christ." But such was their attachment to the ancient religion, that they not only refused to hear this messenger, but conspired to put him to death. Consequently, as he journeyed near the Heugins o' Watley, he was waylaid and seized by a band of rude barbarians. Seeing that his end was come, he craved a few moments' respite for prayer. This being granted, the priest kneeled down and prayed that since the people would not hear his doctrine for the benefit of their souls, there might a fountain flow from his grave for the healing of their bodies. Here the good man was killed, and here on the solitary hillside he was buried; but from his grave their burst forth in perennial flow the healing fountain of Yelabrön.

All persons taking water from this spring brought an offering of three stones, or it might be three coins. Hence at the head of the spring a large cairn of stones has been collected, and I remember when a boy finding old Danish coins there.

When water was brought from this well for sick folk, the journey was made between the hours of sunset and sunrise, and generally the person that bore the medicinal water obtained an inkling of the patient's chance to recover. It might be they heard a *gaenfore* or saw a *feyness*; a white mouse or a black fowl might cross their path. Water from this well must not touch the ground; hence the vessel containing it was generally set on the top of a millstone or *knockin' stane*.

A person likely to die was said to be *fey*, and a *gaenfore* or *feyness* was a prelude of death. Numerous things—both sights and sounds—were said to forebode death in a house or neighbourhood. For example, a cock crowing at an unseason-

Folk-Lore

able hour of the night, the seeing of an owl or a corncrake, a rainbow having both its ends inside a "toon dyke," were all looked upon as evil omens.

Hearing certain sounds in old wood, called a *shaek*, foreboded important events. These sounds are doubtless produced by tiny insects in the wood, but our superstitious forefathers heard them as the voice of Fate. A sound like the ticking of a watch was called a "marriage shaek," a vibrating sound a "flitting shaek," and a dropping sound a "dead shaek."

The following names were applied to diseases of animals :—

Turkasöt—The skin adhering firmly to the back.
Lungasöt—Form of bronchitis.
Whirkabis or *Bulga*—Dropsical swelling in the throat.
Sturdie—Water on the brain.
Yogar or *Spaegie*—Rheumatic affections of the joints.
Sköl—A mouth disease in horses.
Gaaners—A mouth disease in cows.
Feerie—An epidemic disease among dogs.

Shetland Folk-Lore

For all these maladies some antidote was found, and may have proved as effectual as some of the modern concoctions of the now-a-days V.S.

The skilful housewife could diagnose her cow's ailments by carefully noting the various tones of sound uttered by the animal in health and disease. The following names were applied to sounds made by a cow:—

Bröl—The ordinary, natural sound.
Gul-bröl—An emphatic or excited *bröl*.
Skröl—A frightened sound.
Umble—A throat sound, as if choking.
Njoag—A nasal sound.
Drund—A moaning sound.

Sounds made by other animals were:

Sneg and *Nikker*—By horses.
Eer, Reein, and *Loadie-grunt*—By the pig.
Nyrr—By the cat.
Peester—By the mouse.
Klaug—By the hen.
Oob—By the seal.
Yarm—By the sheep.

There were several superstitious notions

connected with the cock. It was exceedingly lucky to possess a black cock. There was a belief that *trows* were quite powerless within sound of its crowing. "A black cock with a red breast had more virtue than a priest."

Women at the time of child-bearing were especially liable to be taken by the *hillfolk*, and hence the midwife was generally an expert in the art of preserving her charge from the *trows*. When a birth was about to take place, it was customary to borrow a black cock to have in the house. The ordinary rooster did not trouble himself to crow save at midnight and in the morning, but the swart bird of which we speak detected the *vaam* of any unseen presence, and announced the same by crowing at any hour. When a cock was heard crowing at an unseasonable time, it was understood that some *fey* person (doomed to die) was within hearing; and if a person had met with any serious fright, the living heart was torn from the breast of the cock, and applied bleeding to the left breast of the individual affected.

The *trows* sometimes rendered themselves visible to ordinary mortals, and are said to have left behind them some of their own domestic utensils, the possession of which was reckoned very lucky.

In a house near a place called Gungsta a wooden cog was captured from a *trowie* wife, and this cog or kit was possessed for generations, and used for milking; and whether the cow was *teed*, *forrow*, or *yield*, the cog was filled to the brim. A cow in full milk is said to be *teed*; in second year's milk, without having a calf, *forrow*; having no milk, *yield*.

A similar vessel, said to have been obtained from the *trows*, was long preserved in the North Isles as a *maet-löm* for any animal supposed to be suffering from the evil eye.

The following legend is told regarding it. A certain goodwife had risen about *da swaar o' simmer dim* to get a little milk for her child. As she entered the byre, she beheld a *trow* milking her cow. She stood spell-bound, unable to speak or move. Presently the *trowie* wife exclaimed:

> "Himpie, hornie, hoy,
> Minnie kum carl mi mug."

Or according to another version:

> "O, when an' döl, da bairn is faaen
> I' da fire an' brunt."

The woman now had power to "sain hersel'," and the *trow* went like lightning out the byre *lum*, dropping the kit as she went.

An old man named Henry Farquhar or Forker is asleep on a bench in the corner of the *butt-end*. In the small hours of the morning he is awakened by the glimmer of a weird light. He sees a *trow* enter carrying a new-born child. In her hand she holds a tiny jar of peculiar workmanship. He tries to "sain himsel'," but is powerless. But on the *bauk* sit two cocks, the one white and the other black. As this strange visitor proceeds to anoint her child with the contents of the jar, the white cock crows, and the *trow* says :

> "The white cock is nae cock,
> Waadie, Waadie,
> I can sit still an' warm me baby."

But presently the black cock crows, and, jumping up, the *trow* exclaims :

> "The black cock is a cock,
> Waadie, Waadie,
> I maun noo flit frae warmin' me baby."

The spell that bound old Farquhar is broken, and, jumping up from his couch, he seizes the jar on the hearthstone. Hence the origin of "Forker's Pig."

This *pig* or jar was made of unglazed clay, holding about a gill. It was preserved with great care, and was fetched here and there to persons supposed to be hurt by *trows*. The last possessor of the said *pig* gave it to the writer several years ago.

SOCIAL LIFE IN OLDEN TIMES.

The young folks of the present generation have little idea of the way in which our forefathers lived. The luxuries and conveniences to which we are accustomed were then unknown. The inhabitants of these islands subsisted almost entirely on their native productions. The harvest of the land, eked out by the harvest of the sea, furnished their sole means of subsistence; and it is no matter for surprise to hear old people speaking of the "scarce years."

Stories have been handed down of the seasons of want and the extreme shifts to which the people were sometimes reduced. Near the sites of old townships enormous quantities of shells, particularly whelks, may be dug up, showing that these have been extensively used as food.

Their supplies were drawn from the crops of oats, bere, potatoes, and cabbage; from the sheep that lived in the scattalds;

and from the fish that swarmed round the shores. It may be said that these still form the staple means of support. True, but we do not use them as our fathers did. We barter them for tea from China and Ceylon, for sugar from the West Indies, for flour ground in Canadian mills, and for fruits and condiments from the shores and islands of the Mediterranean. We do not clothe ourselves with the warm fleece of the sheep, but exchange it for flimsy fabrics from the mills of Manchester, printed calicoes, and bright metal trinkets.

On a Shetland croft of last century the dwelling-house, barn, and byre were built together, so that access could be had to all parts from within. Ingress to and egress from the dwelling was commonly through the byre. When this was not the case, the door was protected by a *töfa*, or porch. The barn was furnished with a kiln for drying corn, built in a corner, and about six feet long by three broad. A few thin lathes, called "kiln trees," lay from side to

Folk-Lore

side. These were covered with a thin layer of *gloy* (straw), on which the corn was spread. The fire burned under the *chylpin-stane* in the kiln *huggie*, and needed

FIG. 11.—*Shetland Hand-Mill.*

constant watching. At the side of the kiln stood a large straw basket, called a *skeb*, in which the corn was rubbed by foot when

Shetland Folk-Lore

dried. On the wall hung a straw mat, called a *flakkie*, on which the corn was winnowed after being thrashed, and to separate the *dumba* before being ground. In the barn also was the hand-mill (Fig. 11), resting on a rude table called a *looder*. This mill was and still is chiefly used for grinding *burstin* (corn dried in a kettle over the fire). Well-made bere *burstin* makes delicious bread.

In the corner of the *butt-end* lay the *knockin' stane* and *mell*, for the purpose of shelling bere, or barley, as a delicacy for *helly* days and Sunday dinners. At the burn close by stood the water-mill (Fig. 12), on which the crop was ground during the *yarrowin*. The mill was driven by a rude, horizontal water-wheel, called a *tirl*. Over the "eye" of the mill was suspended an apparatus through which the corn passed, consisting of a *happer*, *shö*, and *klapper*. In a corner of the *looder* stood a *toyeg* (a small straw basket), containing as much corn as would be a *hurd o'*

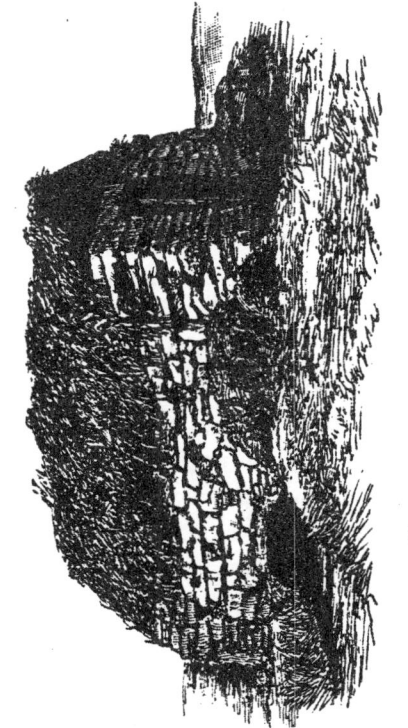

FIG. 12.—*Shetland Water-Mill.*

burstin. This was the annual offering to the Water Neugle, in order to insure the good services of his godship. When this was neglected, the Neugle would sometimes grasp the *tirl* and stop the mill, and could only be dislodged by dropping a firebrand down by the *lightnin' tree*. The ground meal was sifted in sieves made of sheep-skin, fastened tightly round a hoop or rim, and perforated with red-hot *reva-twirries* (straightened out fish hooks). When sifted, the meal fell into three divisions—meal, groats, and *ootsiftins*, from the last of which that delicious food called *sooans*, and that healthy tonic beverage known as *swats*, are made.

In the yard near the *stiggie* was often to be seen a small *skroo* of corn, standing apart from the rest. This was the annual offering set apart to Broonie, a household deity whose good services were thus secured, particularly in protecting the corn yard and thatch roofs during the storms of winter. No article of clothing

Folk-Lore

was ever devoted to this imaginary being, for—

"When Broonie got a cloak or hood,
He did his master nae mair good."

One of the most interesting appendages of the croft was the sheep *krö*. Here lads and lasses met to *roo* the sheep and mark the lambs, and sometimes in scarce years to *kavel* the lambs. The *krö* is a small round enclosure into which sheep are driven, and to facilitate the driving small branch dykes run out in two directions from the *krö*. These were termed *soadin* or *rexter* dykes, and sometimes *steugies*. In the *krö* the uniformity of colour observable in other flocks is wanting. Here is a blending of numerous shades, black, white, brown, and grey being the most common, while there is a sprinkling of *blyeag* (dirty white), *shaela* (steel gray), *moorit* (the colour of brown peat), and *catmuggit* (having the belly of a different colour). Everyone knew his own sheep by the marks cut in their ears. No two persons could have the same mark. If anyone got a lamb from another, an *oobregd* (off-break) mark must be put thereon. The various sheep marks had names by which they were known, *bits*, *crooks*, *fidders*, and *shöls* indicating different cuts in the ear. The people were constantly among the hills tending their sheep and *kyndin* the cows; and there was scarcely a spot that was not called by some appropriate name of Norse origin, such beautiful characteristic names as *Grunna Blaet* (the green spot), *Swarta Blaet* (the black or dark spot), *Gulla Hammar* (the yellow rocks), *Rora Klaet* (the red rocks). Many others might be named. Animals too had names, generally derived from their colour, such as *Sholma* (white face), *Sponga* (spotted), *Greema* (white spotted on the cheeks), *Rigga* (having a stripe running along the back), *Cullya* (polled), etc. These names all end in *a*, and denote the feminine gender. The masculine of animal names ended in *i* or *e*.

Folk-Lore

Since there was little or no imported grain, meal was a scarce commodity, and had to be most economically used, whether baked into *brönies*, *bannocks*, or *kröls*. Cabbage entered largely into the winter dietary, in such preparations as *lang kale*, *short kale*, and *tartanpurry*. Tea was almost unknown. The *blaandie-kaulik* and the *swatsi-swaarik* did duty instead of the golden tips of Ceylon. But fish was the chief article of food. Every house almost had a *skjo* (open built hut for drying fish), in which fish was stored for future use. Fish for home consumption was seldom salted, but preserved in various ways, such as *reested* (dried inside with fire and smoke), *blawn* (dried in the wind), and *gozened* (dried in the sun).

The liver of the fish was extensively used in a fresh state, and entered into the formation of numerous nutritious dishes, such as *stap*, *gree'd fish*, *liver heads*, *liver muggies*, *krampies*, *krappin*, *mooguildin*, *hakka muggies*, and *slot*. To this extensive use of fish livers may be attributed the hardihood of the old Shetlander, and the almost perfect immunity from some fatal forms of disease that afflict us in these days. One cannot but feel sad to see some poor, diseased form of humanity advised as a last resource to "try cod liver oil." Had the dietary afore-mentioned been attended to, the disease calling for fish oil treatment would probably never have been engendered.

But, alas, our inshore handline fishing is a thing of the past. The trawlers are killing the goose that laid the golden egg.

A WHALSAY MAN'S SOLILOQUY.

"O, for da days whan codlins wis rife,
Whan stap an' gree'd fish wis da joy o' mi life,
Whan frae moarnin' ta e'enin' on da sheek o' a gjo
Ye could ha' pokket or drawn da fill o' a skjo.
Dan a' kinds o' sma' fish adoarned da raeps,
An' piltik an' sillok lay soornin' in haeps;
Dere wis kippoks o' haddocks an' weel-speeted hoes;
Heads dow'd, vam'd an draven, affectin' da nose;

Folk-Lore

Dere wis langies o' turbot 'at hang i' da reest,
An' hoe eggs resemblin' a truncher o' beest;
An' beautiful muggies, spleetin' wi gree,
Da bite o' your teeth sent a spoot i' your e'e.
Dat wis da stuff for greasin' your t'roat,
Or aetin' benon a kettle o' slot!
If a body haed risen ta look at da watch,
Ta spit i' da fire wis as guid as a match.
Baith aald folk an' young folk, frae Sodom ta Clate,
Spent da lang winter night in rivin' hard skate.
If it is ordeen'd I never sall see
Da chauds an' da krampies, da oceans o' gree,
Dis I can say—I'll remember forever
Da blessin' 'at cam frae da fish an' its liver."

Let us now return to the crofter's house. It is night, and the old man has returned from the handline fishing. His *böddie* is well stocked with fish. He sits by the round fire, with a *baet o' gloy* or a *kirvie o' floss*, winding it may be *simmonds* or *gurdastöries* for his *maeshies* and *rivakessies*. In the corner in past the fire, (which was on the middle of the floor), on the *lit-kettle*, sits an old grandmother or a "quarter wife" rocking the cradle, or

Shetland Folk-Lore

holding in her lap a *ramished* bairn, which she soothes by singing :

> " Husha baa baet dee,
> Minnie is gaen ta saet dee,
> Fur ta pluck an' fur ta pu',
> An' fur ta gadder luckies' oo,
> Fur ta buy a bull's skin
> Ta row peerie weerie in."

Or, it may be, in more dolorous tones she sings :

> " Husha baa, Minnie's daaty,
> We sall pit da trows awa';
> Broonie sinna git da bairn,
> If he comes da cocks 'ill craw."

If the fractious child has been silenced by the mention of Broonie, it will be dandled with lightsome lilt as granny sings :

> " Upride, upride, upride da bairn ;
> Ride awa, ride awa, ride awa da Neugle ;
> Haud dee tongue, cuddle doon,
> An' du sall git a buggle.

No person is idle. The grown-up females of the household are busily engaged preparing wool for the loom, which is to be made into underclothing for the

Folk-Lore

family, or dyed with *blue-lit, old man skrottie, korkalit,* or *yellowin' girs*, as suiting to the goodman of the house or dresses for the females.

Perhaps some neighbour lad has called to "hadd him oot o' langour," to hear the old man's *klak* news, or what is more likely, to spend the evening in sweet companionship with the oldest lass. The common pastime for such occasions was "layin' up guddiks," *i.e.*, propounding riddles. The simple pastimes were of native origin, but considerable ingenuity was shown in weaving out of the scant material at hand a programme for an evening's entertainment.

I shall here record a few *guddiks* (riddles) and other fireside amusements that were used by our forefathers in their social gatherings, to while away the long winter evenings. I believe the only specimen of the kind now extant, and of Norse origin, is that mentioned in Dr. Jacobsen's "Shetland Dialect." I remember hearing

Shetland Folk-Lore

it in Norwick, Unst, about forty years ago, but I had quite forgotten it until it was reproduced in the valuable work referred to. It is as follows :

> " Fira hunga, fira gunga,
> Fira staad ipo skö,
> Twa veestra vaig a bee,
> An' een comes atta driljandie."

This riddle, as explained by Dr. Jacobsen, has reference to the cow, viz. :

> " Four hanging—the teats,
> Four going—the legs,
> Four standing upwards—horns and ears,
> And one comes behind shaking—the tail."

I have heard in several parts of Shetland what appears to be an Anglicised variant of the same :

> " Four hingers and four gangers,
> Twa luckers and twa crookers,
> Twa laavers and ae dillie-daunder."

Again, here is another riddle, the meaning of which is a woman milking a cow :

> " Tink-tank, twa in a bank,
> Ten about four."

Folk-Lore

"I grew wi' da coo, yet was made by a man,
I böre till his moo what boiled i' da pan."

The meaning of this is a horn spoon. In olden times these were of native manufacture. They were often termed *gaeppies* on account of their size, which required the mouth to be widely opened.

"I ha'e three feet, bit not ae haand;
I ha'e five maids at my commaand;
I ha'e ae e'e, bit canna see;
I ha'e twa haerts in my bodie;
I go fu' faster than a mill,
An' yet my feet are staandin' still;
An' whether I am in or oot,
My guts are always me withoot."

This is a perfect description of a Shetland spinning wheel. The "guts" referred to the wheel-band, which was made of the intestines of sheep, and was called *term*.

"Four-neukit, tail-teukit,
An' teeth oot o' number."
Answer—Wool cards.

"What is it 'at tears een anidder a' day,
An' sleeps in een anidder's airms a' nicht."
Answer—Wool cards.

Shetland Folk-Lore

"What is it that goes through a rock, through a reel, through an aald spinny wheel, through a sheep's shank bane."

Answer—A web of cloth.

"I gaed atween twa wids,
An' I cam' atween twa watters."

Answer—One going to the well with wooden buckets.

"Peerie fool (fowl) featherless,
New come oot o' Paradise,
Fleein' ower da mill dam,
Catch me if du be a man."

Answer—A snowflake.

"Hookatee, krookatee, foo rins du?
Clipped tail every year, why spör's du?"

This is what the meadow and the brook said to each other.

"Roond like a millstane,
Lugged like a cat,
Staandin' upo' three legs—
Can du guess dat?"

Answer—A kettle.

"Twa grey grumphies lay in ae sty,
Da maer dey get, da maer dey cry;
Da less dey get, da stiller dey lie."

Answer—The millstones.

Folk-Lore

"I gaed oot ae moarnin' in May,
I fan a thing in a cole o' hay,
It wis nedder fish, flesh, feather, or bane,
Bit I kept it till it could gaeng its lane."

Answer—An egg.

These may serve as specimens of Shetland riddles. There was scarcely anything either about the house, within or without the house, that was not made the subject of a *guddik*.

Another favourite pastime was *going in wads* (forfeits). There were various forms practised in this game. I shall mention one that I remember seeing in Unst, and which, I doubt not, is very old.

The young people are seated round the open fireplace. A piece of straw, or better still, of dried dockweed, say about eight inches long, is bent in the form of an acute triangle. Both the ends are lighted in the fire and begin to burn slowly, something like a cigar. It is now carefully balanced at the angular point on another straw held perpendicularly in the hand of No. 1, who exclaims: "Wha'll buy my jantle Jockie belaand?" No. 2 answers: "What if he dees i' dy ain haand?" No. 2 replies: "Da back sall bear da saddle baand, thro' moss, thro' mire, thro' mony a laand, that gars my jantle Jockie dee or get a faa." The burning triangle is now handed to No. 2, who repeats the same formula together with No. 3, and so on to the next; and anyone in whose hand the "gentle Jockie dees" (fire goes out) or "gets a faa" (falls) that one is in a *wad*, and is punished (?) by kissing every person of the opposite sex present, or by answering a number of dark questions, commonly having reference to love and courtship.

Straw was put to numerous uses by the old Shetlander. It was food and bedding for his cattle. It thatched his roof and formed his couch at night. The very seat on which he sat was made of this humble material. It furnished another favourite subject for evening amusement. No. 1 of the party begins by asking No. 2: "What

Folk-Lore

öse is strae for?" No. 2 replies: "Strae is for mony a guid öse, particularly ta mak' saat cuddies (small baskets for salt) o'. What öse is strae for?" No. 3 answers: "Strae is for mony a good öse, if it wis bit ta mak' a wizzie o'. What öse is strae for?" And so on, round and round, until someone at last failed to find a use for straw that had not been previously mentioned.

SHETLAND FESTIVITIES.

We who live in these days have our social gatherings, our picnics and soirees, our balls and club meetings, etc. These names were unknown to our forefathers. Yet we learn that they were a highly social people. It was in their nature to rejoice with them that rejoiced and to weep with them that wept. The fishermen tarried for one another, and the husbandman did not consider his own work completed until his neighbour's crop was in the yard. They had not acquired that selfishness which is an outgrowth of our so-called modern civilisation whose policy is: "Man mind dysel', an deil tak' the hinmost." The *upstaander* and the *yarmer* had not then learned to quarrel over a "mug o' lū watter."

In the festivities of the olden time there seems to have been special respect paid to the number three. For example, during the season the crew of a *haf* boat had three feasts, viz.: the *Doon-drawin'* at Beltane; the *Johnsmas* at Midsummer, when they supped the "milgruel kits"; and the *Foy* at Lammas, when the fishing closed.

When births, marriages, and deaths occurred, there were three feasts in connection with each. On the occasion of a birth there was the *Blithe-feast*, when the child was born; the *Fittin'-feast*, when the mother came to the fire and resumed her duties; and the *Christenin'*, when the child was baptised. In connection with a marriage there were the *Spörin'*, the *Contract*,

Folk-Lore

and the *Bridal*, which commonly "stood" three days. *Spör* means to ask or enquire —hence the *spörin'* was the occasion when the bridegroom asked in a formal way the consent of the bride's parents. Even at the final and most solemn event of life the three feasts were still observed, viz,, the *Kistin'*, the *Funeral*, and the *Condolin'*.

Winter was the chief season of festivity. As a rule all marriages took place during the three winter moons.

Arrangements were made about the beginning of November for holding the Hallowmas banquets. The young lads banded themselves together in squads and went *hoosamylla* (from house to house), as maskers, commonly called *gröliks*. They received offerings of money, *burstin brönies*, legs of *vivda*, or dried *sparls*. When the rounds of the district had been completed, they repaired to a neighbouring barn with their sweethearts, and the banquet was spread. They amused themselves with such games as *hunt-da-slipper*, *wads*, and *haand-de-kroopin.* The singing of good old ballads and the "laying up" of *guddiks* gave variety to the entertainment. But more frequently these guileless maidens and their happy lovers tripped with lightsome lilt the old Shetland reels, such as "Nippin' Grund," "Da Brunt Scones o' Voe," "Da Scalloway Lasses," "Shak'-'im-troose," "Kale an' Knocked Corn," etc.

There is a desire in the human mind to pry into the future, and even at the present day, in this land of Kirks and Bibles, you may see jolly lads in H.M. uniform and braw young lasses patronising the professional cup and card reader. The chief object of the Hallowmas sports of the olden time was to get a peep on the other side of the curtain that separates the present from the future. I shall relate a few of the old customs practised at the Hallowmas festival.

Drappin' Glasses.—This was performed by dropping a small portion of the white of an egg into a glass of water. The forms assumed prognosticated the future in matters of love, fortune, and death.

Tyin' the Kale Stock.—For this purpose the young folks went blindfold into the kale-yard, and each one tied his or her garter round the first kale-stock they touched, and the number of shoots on the *kastik*, which was counted in the morning, was a forecast of the family of the future.

Castin' the Clew.—This was a more elaborate affair, and required a considerable amount of nerve for its performance. At the dead of night one person alone went to the water-mill, and getting on the roof, dropped a ball of worsted in through the *lum*, holding fast the end. Then the operator on the roof began to rewind the clew into another ball, repeating the while in a steady tone: "Wha hadds my clew end?" Then a voice from out the dark mill was expected to answer the name of the future husband or wife.

Turnin' the Sleeve.—This was per-

Shetland Folk-Lore

formed at the hour of midnight. A person wishing to read the future by this means went all alone and unseen, and wet their shirt sleeve in a burn over which a corpse had been borne. They next retired to a barn or other outhouse and kindled a fire, hanging up the wet shirt as if to dry. The owner of the shirt now retires to the opposite end of the barn and lies down to wait. As the hours pass away, the dying embers cast weird shadows on the walls. Presently, amid the gloom and fitful flicker an apparition is seen flitting across the floor and silently turning the wet sleeve. This is none other than the phantom of the future husband or wife. If nothing is seen and the shirt remains unturned, the prier into futurity may look forward to a life of single bliss. But sometimes it was said that the dark outline of a coffin was seen, warning the poor watcher to prepare for another world.

Fathomin' the Skroo.—As has already

Folk-Lore

been stated, in olden times a small stack, commonly bere, was set apart as an annual offering to *Broonie*. Now, one went blindfold into the corn yard and fathomed this *skroo*, three times with the sun and thrice *widdershins*, and at the last turn they were supposed to clasp in their embrace the form of their lover—perhaps Broonie himself.

Siftin' Siller.—The operator in this case went alone into a room having a window, and placing a looking-glass opposite, he took his stand between the window and the mirror, having his back turned towards the window. Then, with three silver coins in a seive, he sifted away, steadfastly gazing at the mirror, in which, be it observed, a view reflected from the window was obtained. While this was going on, he expected to behold, passing before his astonished gaze in a sort of panoramic order, the whole of his future life.

Passin' the Harrow.—This was a per-

Shetland Folk-Lore

formance seldom practised, except by some person of a "deil-may-care" disposition, for while the other Hallowmas sports had for their object merely the forecasting of matters matrimonial, this was supposed to unfold the future, even the spirit-world; and the person who had the hardihood to "go i' da harrow" never revealed what they either saw or heard, and always warned others not to try such a trick. The performance was very simple. Three harrows were placed, some distance apart, outside the open fodder door of an old barn, and at the hour of midnight a person went blindfold into the yard and passed back foremost over each harrow in turn, thence through the barn window, and at the end of this journey he was supposed to fall into a sort of trance and hear and see unutterable things.

When Hallowmas was past, the people set themselves in right earnest to their winter duties. Handline or *klak* fishing was practised when weather permitted, and

Folk-Lore

the *skjos* were well stocked with fish for the approaching Yule festivities. During stormy weather the men were occupied in making numerous articles for domestic use from straw, such as *kessies, mael böddies, skebs, toyegs, flakkies, rivakessies, simmond-chairs, saat kuddies*, etc.

The women were occupied carding and spinning wool, although the manufacture of *wadmil* had long ceased. The making of cloth for home wear was universally practised, and in almost every township there could be found the professional *wobster* (weaver), whose busy shuttle seldom stopped the livelong winter. Here and there were persons of artistic skill whose business it was to *taat* bed rugs with wool dyed in *blue lit, skrottie, kurka-lit, aald man*, or *yellowin' girs*. The social disposition of the people led them to spend much of their time, especially the long winter evenings, in each other's houses, whiling away the time in telling stories of the sea, tales of adventures with

Shetland Folk-Lore

trows and witches, stories of smugglers, wrecks, and press-gang, together with more rational affairs both general and domestic. No finer specimen of the home talk of the olden time can be given than is contained in "Shetland Fireside Tales," and the "Fireside Cracks" of the *Shetland Times*.

To the young and gay winter wore slowly away, and many a time and oft did old matrons answer the question, "Is it lang ta Yule?" At last the 20th of December (O.S.) dawns, and a look of joy and expectancy may be seen on every face. The "muckle wheel" is taken off the *butt* wall, and *cairds* and *knuck*s, *sweeries* and *reels*, are laid aside for a season. The handmill is taken off the *sile* and turned upside down on the *looder*, lest during the *helly days* it should be driven *widdershins* by witch and warlock. The Yule peats are carried in, and a *reested* cow's head or sheep's head is laid in steep for the Byaena-Sunday *brose*.

Folk-Lore

This is Tammasmas E'en, and the day following is Tammasmas Day, in which no manner of work can be done.

> "Ta shape or shu,
> Ta bake or brew,
> Ta reel a pirm
> Or wind a clew,
> A lö soolpaltie
> Will tak you."

Even—

> "Da bairn i' da midder's wime
> 'Ill mak' woefu' döl,
> If wark be wrought on Tammasmas night,
> Five nights afore Yule."

At last Yule morning dawns. This is the chief festival of the season. At other times there may be scant, but now there is no want. It is true, everything is of native origin and simplicity, but still a wonderful variety may be seen. Every person, old and young, wears something new on Yule morning. The round peat fire blazes to the *crook-bauk*. The *kollie* (Fig. 13), well fed with *sillok* oil, hangs on the *raep*, illuminating the *butt-end*. The *ben* room is lighted with an irregular tallow dip, stuck in the neck of an empty Dutch "krook."

The day is spent in feasting, and at

FIG. 13.—*Shetland Kollie.*

night the service of the local fiddler is called for, and the merry-go-round of the Shetland *Rant* is kept up from house to

Folk-Lore

house until Four-an'-twenty Day (18th January, O.S.), when the exhausted larders reminded the people that it was time to resume the more stern duties of life.

The last festival of winter was Fastern's E'en, a movable feast, about the beginning of February.

> " First comes Candlemas,
> An' dan da new mön,
> An' dan comes Fastern's E'en
> Whin a' da guid is döne."

PROVERBS AND SAYINGS

PROVERBS AND SAYINGS

THERE are many old witty sayings used in the islands and familiar to every Shetlander. In many instances the wise saws quoted in this chapter belong to the traditions of the remote past, or are of native origin, while in the case of proverbs imported in more recent times, it will be seen that they have suffered a sea-change and acquired a local flavour.

A man whose mind is enlarged by education and the general information derived from books, and who possesses a command of language, expresses his ideas in his own words, whereas the illiterate man uses the proverbial expressions which tradition has handed down and daily usage rendered familiar, and he justifies his action or verifies his argument with a proverb.

The following old saws were jotted down by me about 30 years ago, while I was lodging in the house of the late Mr. James Manson, of Scraefield, Unst. He was born about the beginning of the century, had a most retentive memory well stocked with folk-lore, and to him I am indebted for many of the sayings. I also received a list from the late Mr. Robert Jamieson, Sandness, which contained several proverbs that were new to me.

The meaning of many of these old sayings is self evident, while it may be said of others that one must live in their environment in order to understand or appreciate them. Many of them throw considerable

Proverbs and Sayings

light on the social life of our ancestors. They show that the Shetlanders were a contented people :

"Better half an egg than a töm doop."
"Better a cauld bite than nae bread."
"Better a moose i' the kale than nae kitchen."

These all breathe of contentment. It was indeed hard for a mother to set her bairns round a "kitchenless" pot, hence the least seasoning was matter for thankfulness.

"It's a guid day that pits aff the night."

Here again the same spirit of content is manifest. The old fisherman had toiled all day without success. Night had come and he returns just "with the supper"— nothing for to-morrow ; but he comforts himself that the wants of to-night have been met by the toils of to-day.

Perhaps he has been in grips with the *baldin* (halibut), and fainly hoped to feast on its *barr cuts*, but just as it came within sight of the boat its last desperate struggle "made up the skoag," and the fisherman is doomed to disappointment; but he comforts himself by saying:

> "There's as guid a fish i' the sea as ever wis ta'en."
> "The sea bids come again."

Further:

> "Better that ae heart breaks than a' the world winders"—

Better patiently to bear one's own troubles alone, than to publish them abroad as material for gossip.

> "When my hat is on, my family is covered."
> "Better loose than ill tethered."
> "It's a silly hen that canna scrape for hersel'."

These are expressions of a disappointed lover, or the spinster doomed to single bliss.

> "Du'll sole dy socks wi' lesser claith."

This saying is given as a rebuke to one who aspires beyond her position.

Several of these old sayings show that the Shetlanders were a people accustomed

Proverbs and Sayings

to penury, which necessitated the practice of the strictest economy :

"If ye döna hain the breer, da bottom 'ill hain itsel'."

That is, it's late time to practice economy when the meal barrel is empty, or in the words of another proverb :

"It's better lang little than shön (soon) naithin'."

"Skeek weel, hae lang."

Skeek signifies to use sparingly, and is similar in meaning to the words *hain* and *haag*.

There were no doubt seasons of prolonged scarcity, and when supplies came at last, the appetite sharpened by hunger made greater demands. Hence the proverb :

"Lang want is nae bread hainin'."

"A body mann fach as they're forn "—

A labourer will work as he's fed. *Fach* is applied to the cultivation of land that had been cropped with potatoes the previous year, and is counted hard work. *Forn* means to be fed.

The wisdom of limiting one's expenditure to their resources is well expressed in the sayings:

"Bake as ye're bodin."
"Cut your claes accordin' to your claith."
"Measure your green accordin' to your gray."

The mistress of the house was looked upon as the *maet-midder*, and hungry bairns did not consider her exhausted larder, and often cried for a *kröl* when the *mael-pock* was empty. Even the head of the house forgot the very limited resources of his better-half. Hence the following old sayings:

"A hungry man is an angry man."
"Hungry dogs never bark weel."
"Hungry bairns greet sair."
"It's a braw wife that brings butt what's no ben."
"The thing can sair dee an' me, that canna sair twa or three."
"They that gi'e me [a] little wid see me livin'."

In olden times the people were largely

Proverbs and Sayings

dependent for food on the milk of their cows and the flesh of their sheep, and he who possessed a number of these useful animals was a man of wealth among his less fortunate neighbours. Hence :

"The pör man's coo never calves oot o' time."
"The raem (cream) o' ae coo's milk is thin."
"The coo milks frae the head" (as she's fed).
"The pör man's sheep are short tailed" (few).
"The pör man's kye are shön kyanded."

The following convey the same meaning as the well-known saying, " Better endure those ills we have, than fly to others that we know not of " :

"Better rue sit than rue flit."
"Every gait haes a mire at the end o' it."
"Better the ill kent than the guid unkent."

"When the wirm moves it's wise ta flit"—

We should be guided by reason. This old saying has reference to the habit observable in Shetland sheep that have access to the seashore from their pasture. They are known to start for the coast at ebb tide to feed on seaweed, and they are said to know the ever-varying time of low water by the movement of a worm or parasite in the fore feet.

"It's dear coft hinney that's sucked oot o' the t'orn (thorn)"

has reference to the difficulty of obtaining a livelihood from the unproductive soil.

"What winna wash, winna wring"

is rather difficult to explain. It conveys the idea that it is vain to strive against overmastering circumstances.

"The wind aye blaws i' da pör man's face."
"The pör man's lot is a leeward tide."

These are very expressive of the struggle against adverse circumstances.

"The pap milk 'ill need ta be oot o' dy nose"—

You will be required to act the man, and he who possesses a manly heart will say:

"I'm no been fed on a steb-midder's kröl."

"A yield soo wis never guid wi' grices"—

A bantering expression having reference

Proverbs and Sayings

to step-mothers or old maids that have charge of children.

"Need mak's a naked man rin."
"Need mak's a man a craft."

These are intelligently explained by the popular saying, "Necessity is the mother of invention."

"The fire burns whaar it's bigged"—

They who undertake the management of affairs that belong to other people, may make up their minds to have an extra share of trouble.

"Better to wile the haand oot o' the wolf's mouth than tear it oot."
"Wiles help weak folk."
"Seldom comes ae ill its lane."
"Soon is a guid hoose skailed."
"Soon is a guid hoose pu'd doon."
"Broken pots in a' pairts."
"Oot o' the fire and into the embers."

All these proverbial expressions are self-explanatory.

A number of the proverbs used by our

forefathers are characteristic of a people who were helpful, obliging, and kind-hearted—borrowing from and lending to each other. In those days the useful implements that minister to the comfort and convenience of every-day life were few and of a rude sort, and these only possessed by the more fortunate. Hence:

"Borrow and lend helps mony a man."
"Gif-gaf mak's guid friends."
"The weel-willed man is the beggar's bridder"—

He who supplies all seekers will soon exhaust his own resources.

The duty of taking care of borrowed articles is taught in the saying:

"Aye let a len come lauchin' hame."

"Tiggers soodna be tarrowers."

Tig means to beg, and *tarrow* signifies to slight or refuse. Hence persons that beg should never be fastidious. Similar to the popular saying:

"It's ill ta look a gift horse i' the mooth."

Proverbs and Sayings

"He that tak's what he haes never wants."

This refers to the person that dislikes to borrow, who, rather than ask for his neighbour's hammer, will drive his nail with the *crook* or even a stone.

Often the man most willing to help lacked the power or the means to do so, and this is very comprehensively expressed in the following proverb:

"The riven sleeve keeps the haand back."

Again:

"They that hae a riven sleeve mann hadd their tongue."

This has a different meaning. The "riven sleeve" here refers to something one would hide, as a fault; hence one must not be censorious of the shortcomings of others who have similar failings.

"It's ill ta gi'e a naked man claes."
"The spillin' haand never wants."
"Better a timmer cap o' my ain, than a siller cup that's borrowed."
"A man may live by a' his kin, but by his neighbour he canna win."

Shetland Folk-Lore

All these explain themselves, and have reference to the habit of borrowing and lending.

Here are a few proverbial expressions that very aptly set forth the law of heredity and natural tendency:

"An ill röt never sprang a guid branch."
"It's ill ta get oot o' the flesh what's bred i' the bane."
"Water 'ill be whaar water haes been."
"Still water haes the warst wirm."
"Still water haes maist mud."
"The aald coo seeks her ain baand."

The power of example and habit are illustrated in the following:

"The aald cock craws an' the young ene learns."
"He that gets in his finger 'ill shön get in his haand."

The universal truth that whatsoever a man soweth that shall he also reap, is very curtly expressed in four syllables—"Sel' dö, sel' hae"; and the dear-bought knowledge acquired in the school of experience is set forth in the adage:

"Skaed (scathe) never made a man rich, but it should mak' 'im wise."

Proverbs and Sayings

Here again are a few proverbs having reference to the habits and upbringing of children :

"Hae boy, rin boy, mak's a guid boy"—

Give a boy food and clothing, and keep him from idleness, and he will grow up to be useful.

"Mony a pelled röl has come to be a guid horse"—

An unpromising youth may become a good man.

"Brunt bairns dread the fire."
"Bairns greet nae langer than they get their will."
"Bairns and föls spaek the truth."
"A close tongue mak's a wise head."
"It's ill ta wint bairns wi' bread, but waar ta wint them aff o' it."
"A short man gets a short faa."
"If bairns grew as they greet, they'd shön be grit."
"Ramished bairns are ill ta please."
"They can dö ill that canna dö guid."
"Tarrowin' bairns are never fat."

Hence a child refusing to eat because he has "ta'en the dorts," or is sulky and peevish, is not likely to grow fat, and is best cured by being subjected to a spell of hunger, for "the mair he tarrows the less he gets."

The following seem to have reference to the other end of life:

"Aald folk are twice bairns, an' hinmost warst ava."
"Better late to learn than never to dö weel."
"Better late to mend than never to dö grace."

Here are a few old expressions that teach the importance of perseverance and industry:

"He that lives on hoop (hope) 'ill die fastin'."
"Wissin' an' waddin' are pör hoose haddin'."
"Glowerin' i' the lum never filled the pot."

These all teach the well-known truth that perseverance is the mother of good luck, and that the man who endeavours has the best chance to succeed. Hence—

"The gaengin' fit aye gets somethin', if it wis bit a broken tae."

The following proverb shows that our ancestors did not always rise above the self-interest so common to human nature:

"Everyene bigs the coal best aboot his ain brönie."

Proverbs and Sayings

The wisdom of counting the cost and completing what one has begun is taught in the proverb :

"It's ill to eat the coo an' wirry on the tail."

"Dö weel bids come again"—

Faithful work secures confidence.

"Lay weel up, tak' weel doon"

teaches the orderly habit of having a place for everything and everything in its place.

"Shör bind, shör find"

is very commonly used. The following story will illustrate its application. In the days of the press-gang there lived in Fetlar a man known as Billy Brown. He was of great physical strength and very fleet of foot. Several attempts had been made to take him, but without success. One misty August night the cutter with the press-gang on board lay becalmed in the Wick o' Grötin'. A picked crew was sent off with instructions to land in Moosie Gjo o' Straand, and proceed to Billy's house under cover of the fog to capture and bring him on board. These instructions were carried out with all possible caution, and the press-gang reached Billy's house at an hour when he and his family were supposed to be asleep. Billy, however, was on the alert, and as his would-be captors entered the *butt* door, he sprang out the *ben* chimney, gaining the yard behind the house at a single bound. But just as he crossed the *stiggie* (stile), he was seized by one of the press-gang who had been left outside on watch. Turning on the man, he seized him with an overmastering grip and quickly tied his hands behind his back with a lamb's tether he happened to have in his pocket. The poor, crestfallen official pleaded to be tied more gently, but Billy's only reply was: "Ha, bridder! he that shör bin's, shör fin's, an 'lauchs whin he lowses."

The following proverbs show that a name either for good or evil has a tendency to stick to one:

Proverbs and Sayings

"Black is the stane that a' man spits on."
"Never may the wal (well) be empty that a'body thinks fu'."
"He that gets the name o' early risin', can lie as lang as he laeks."

The following sayings are more difficult to classify :

"Everyene röses the förd as he fin's it."
"Everyene röses the gyurd as he gets it."

Röse means to praise; *förd* signifies a find, something to be carried away ; and *gyurd* is a gift or reward. Hence the meaning conveyed by these expressions is that everyone speak of things as they find them.

"Show me the calf, but no the cog."

This expression is used as a reply to a boastful braggart.

"It's ill to break a strae and look at baith its ends."
"Hairy butter 'ill dö for siddie bread."
"Better to wear out than rust out."
"Better to hae the finger aff than aye blödin'."
"Beauty is but skin deep."
"Nane sae deaf as they that winna hear."
"Boil stanes in butter an' the brö 'ill be guid."

"They that buy beef, buy banes."
"Every cock is pertest on his ain midden head."
"The soo dreams as shö wid (would)."

The last is used banteringly to persons who strongly advocate their own interests.

"The drukken man aye haes the drukken penny."

"Ill news is like a fitless heathercow"—

Evil tidings travel fast, like a tuft of dry heather before the wind.

"Nae news is guid news"

is the expression of an anxious wife or sister awaiting the return of an absent breadwinner. Another old saying has it:

"There's hope frae the door, but nane frae the grave."

"There's nae lee behint a lang-backed sea."

This is a fisherman's proverb, and means that the rolling waves afford no shelter from the storm.

"Ye may gaeng farther an' fare warse."
"They that hae mael an' a tree (stick), can mak' gruel (porridge) i' the sea."
"They that live langest 'ill see farthest."

Proverbs and Sayings

"Far-come fools (birds) hae fine feathers"

teaches that strangers, however fair to appearance, are not to be taken into confidence until we know somewhat of their character.

"Föls (foolish persons) soodna see half-döne wark."
"Föls soodna hae shappin' sticks."
"Föls are better to be flattered than fought."

It was customary in Shetland for sons to marry and take their wives into their father's house, and often two or even three families might be found under one roof. But it generally happened that such families did not live in that harmony which ought to pervade the domestic circle, and here are a few old sayings having reference to this condition of things:

"Freends 'gree best at a distance."
"Freends 'gree best wi' a knowe atween them."
"There's nae hoose grit enough for twa guidwives."
"Twa wives in ae hoose are shör ta live laek cat an' moose."
"See your neighbours every day, an' your freends on Yule day."

Shetland Folk-Lore

"It's ill ta drook a laughin' guest."

A brand standing by itself in the fire was called a guest; a smoking brand betokened an unwelcome guest, while a bright brand meant a friend. The coming of the unwelcome guest might be prevented by pouring water on the brand, but care was needed lest the act should bring misfortune on a friend, who might fall into a mire or burn.

"Glig (quick) is the guest's ee."
"They can tell a tale that canna bear a burden"
—(refers to children).
"It's a pert beggar that goes by ae door."
"Everyday vitchers (visitors) are tiresome guests."

A greedy, grasping, overreaching nature is referred to in the following:

"Guid is laithe (weary) o' the greedy man."
"Gi'e an inch and tak' an ell."
"The mair we hae, the mair we want."
"Du wid skin a midge for her tallow."
"Du wid gaeng atween the lempit an' the stane."

"The glyed (squinting) gunner never made a fat pot."
"He thrives best that never sees his laird's reek."

Proverbs and Sayings

"He that winna when he can, sanna when he may."
"He that's first at the hill sits whaar he will."
"He that gaengs unbidden sits unsaired."
"Justice never köst (threw) his rider."
"It's ill to drive a willin' horse."
"It's no ill döne a man döes to himsel'."
"It's no an ill straik a dog gets wi' a bane."
"Open doors, dogs gaeng ben."
"The deil is aye kind to his ain."
"The fat piece is shön cutted."
"Seldom lies the best piece till hinmost."
"They that come last must tak' what's left."
"There's mony a change in a simmer dim, lat alane in a winter night."
"They spo (prophesy) weel that ken."

"They sail fast that sit at hame"—

They that anxiously wait for the fisherman's return do not take into account the numerous causes for his delay.

"Let be for let be."

This saying or an equivalent will doubtless be found wherever there is a language. The Shetland version runs thus: "Lat be for lat be, as Robbie Glen said to the otter." Now, who Robbie Glen was I am not able to say. I have heard that he belonged to Delting, but there is no doubt he was a real person. Like most Shetland crofters, he owned a number of sheep, and as was his custom, he went out one morning to look for some that were straying. As he trudges over the snow-clad hills, what does he spy but the *bröd o' dratsie* (the footmarks or trail of an otter). Over hill and glen with eager step he follows the *bröd* until its end at the entrance to a *yarff* (hole in the moor) near the side of a burn. The *hadd* is too narrow to allow Robbie to enter and beard the otter in his den. He must dislodge him, and this is done by setting fire to a bundle of dry heather placed in the mouth of the *yarff*. The smoke entering the recess is very offensive to the amphibious creature, and he hastens to escape; but Robbie is on the alert, and throws himself on the poor beast. The struggle is short and severe. The poor otter is stunned with repeated blows and laid aside as dead, while Robbie has received a bite in the left thumb. A

Proverbs and Sayings

few hairs are pulled from the otter's tail and applied to Robbie's wounded member, and slinging his prey by the tail over his shoulder, he marches homeward, well pleased with his success. Now, it appears that the otter had not been dead as was supposed, for all at once he seizes Robbie's hip with a death-grip. Robbie tugs and pulls, but all in vain; and at last, goaded to desperation with pain, he runs to an overhanging brae, against which he places his back, pressing with all his might, while he exclaims: "Noo, bridder, lat be for lat be."

I said that Robbie took some hair from the otter's tail and applied to his finger. It was believed that the best antidote against the effects of the bite of a dog or otter was a hair from the animal's tail. Hence the saying:

"Tak' a hair o' the tek (dog) that bett dee."

"It's ill to follow a bröd (spoor) ipo' flecked ground"—

When the snow is in patches, as is the

case during thaw, it is difficult to trace footprints.

"Ye're a' ae swine's spik (fat)"—
You are all one family; akin to the Scottish expression, "Ye're a' ae 'oo."

"Du only needs a hair ta mak a tether o'"
is applied to one given to exaggeration.

"It's ill ta sit inonder drap, lat alane wi' underwatter"—
It is uncomfortable when the roof drops, but worse when the foundations let in water. Hence, it's hard to endure two evils. Another old saying shows that such is often the lot of man, for

"Seldom comes ae ill withoot a twin."

"Ye'll no get blöd oot o' a stane"—
Akin to "It's ill to get breeks aff o' a Hielanman."

"Auld springs bring nae price."

Here springs refer to music, and the inference is that one gets tired of what they have often heard.

Proverbs and Sayings

"Du dösna bite sae sair as du girns"

refers to one who, under a rough exterior, has a kindly heart.

"They're wilt that wales"

has reference to the difficulty often experienced in choosing among many things.

"It's a willin' will that leads a man to the lady's hoose."

Will signifies to lose one's way as in a fog, and when a man arrives at the house of his sweetheart, pretending he has *wilt* (lost his way), it is understood to be a willing accident. Of lovers they say:

"They hae mony a errand i' da Ha' that bids the lady guid-day."

"There's mair i' dy sheeks as i' dy breeks"

is applied to any braggart who pretends to do what he cannot accomplish.

"There's mony a brave lad on the head o' a dead fish."

This saying doubtless had its origin in connection with whale hunting, and is applicable to one who shows off his bravery when the danger is past.

The following proverbs I have not been able to classify:

"There's aye watter whaar the staig smores."
"Cleanliness is nae pride, an' dirt is nae mournin'."
"Decency is a debt, but Gudeliness a duty."
"It's ill for the rake to come after the besom."
"It's pör times when the dog licks the cat's nose for breakfast."
"It's guid swimmin' when others hold up the head."
"It's a silly hog that canna carry his ain fleece."
"It's little wirt that's no wirt the askin' o'."
"Tanks is pör pay, but it's better than naethin'."
"An ill race is soon run."
"They that meanly sit richly warm."
"The pinched haand haes a caald heart."
"It's a dirty fool (bird) that files its ain nest."
"Better ta keep weel than mak' weel."
"He lauchs in his sleeve that haes the inplay."
"He'll feel whaar his liver lies that andows wi' leeward tide."
"Pör flaichs (fleas) bite sair."
"A fat Yule mak's pör Fastern E'en."
"They that gae wi' the ska 'ill get wi' the scabbart."
"They like ill the face that picks aff the nose."
"A guid paet year wis never a ill maet year."

Proverbs and Sayings

"I'll no wirry upo' kliers"

means "I'll speak my mind freely"; and of slanderers it is said:

"Ye may lock afore a haand t'ief, bit no afore a tongue t'ief."

"The mair dirt the mair luck"

has reference to a fisherman's superstition that it is unlucky to wash out his boat during the fishing season.

"It's guid ta hae a freend, an' no pluck oot his een"—

One should be careful not to make frequent and excessive demands on a generous friend.

"If ye döna tak' gaengers, riders may gae by."

This was the reply of a young lady whose friends objected to her marriage with one whom they considered below her station in life.

"The ill-vicked coo haes short horns"—

Persons of a tyrannical disposition are sometimes deprived of the power to hurt.

Shetland Folk-Lore

"Whaar there's tuss there's buss."

Tuss and *tuk* are old Shetland expressions used to denote broken parts or refuse of hay, straw, etc. *Buss* is bedding for an animal, and is always applied to material used by a bird for building its nest; and the inference of the proverb is that one having numerous things passing through his hands is likely to succeed in "feathering his nest."

"Mony a corp gaengs ta the kirkyard, bit few come frae it."

This is used when the unexpected happens.

"Stramp upo' the snail, an' shö'll stick oot her horns"—

Akin to "The worm will turn when trod upon." "Provocation is enough to make a wise man mad."

"The stane that lies no i' your gaet, breaks no your taes"

refers to the folly of meddling with matters that do not concern us.

Proverbs and Sayings

"Shö (shoe) brö is warm"

is identical with

"Better ill shod than barefitted."
"Better a wet mitten than a caald haand."

"The hoose draps söt (soot)"—

A phrase used as a hint to be cautious in speaking in the hearing of talebearers or children.

"Better what's been than what'll never be."

Two old cronies have met. They knew each other once, though they have long been parted. They wish to renew their friendship over a glass. They drink each other's health in such terms as—"Here's ta dee," "It's better what's been than what'll never be."

"The priest preaches for his ain profit"

is a proverb of general application. The clergy in Shetland have never suffered from the disadvantage of being exalted into a position placing them beyond the reach of criticism, and the patriotic Shetlander says when he sums up the advantages the islands have derived from being severed from Norway:

> "A' the guid we ever got frae Scotland wis dear mael an' greedy ministers."

An old, forgotten custom is commemorated in the following proverb:

> "Ye'll no forget da stane whaar ye got a sair bane."

This refers to the custom of riding the scattald marches, on which occasion a boy got a flogging at each march stone to stimulate his memory.

The last of these old saws I will quote is one I heard many years ago from my friend, Mr. James S. Angus. It survives in the old Norse tongue, and is almost as old-fashioned in sentiment as it is in language, but it breathes the true Old Norse spirit and is full of the wisdom of our forefathers:

> "*Gött a taka gamla manna ro.*"

Or, as Dr. Jakobsen has rendered it:

> "It is good to take old men's advice."

THE LAMMAS FOY

THE LAMMAS FOY

EVERY year about old Lammas the *haf* fishing came to a close. The boats were then hauled up on the green and *whumbled* in their winter *böls*. But before the crew finally broke up for the season, the *Foy* (feast) was held, generally in the skipper's house. To this feast every man brought his wife, and if single his sister or sweetheart.

Although the luxuries of modern times were then unknown, yet the *foy* table was laden with substantial fare. Home-made scones, *burstin brönies*, and *sonsie* pancakes, together with an ample supply of fresh butter and eggs, made good eating. A *reested* (smoked) ham or a few legs of *vivda* gave variety to the bill of fare. On the table stood a couple of Dutch *krooks*, the contents of which cheered the hearts of those weather-beaten sons of toil.

The conversation, as may be supposed, turned chiefly on the fishing, each man recounting his experiences of the perils of the deep, and the hairbreadth escapes he had made. The wives, too, were relating to each other their own or some neighbour's experience with *trows* and witches, and their numerous seasons of anxious waiting while their goodmen were at sea. One of the oldest women was generally called upon to "cast a cup" for the young men, who were anxious to get a peep into the future, particularly in matters of love, and who were generally gratified by hearing of courtships, *spòrins*, and bridals.

As the contents of the *krook* was handed round, the conversation became

The Lammas Foy

more general and noisy. Healths were drunk in warm terms:

"Here's ta dee, boy, as mony a blissin' as we hae crossed a saat watter drap tagedder."

"Gude hadd His haand ower da corn, an' open da mooth o' da gray fish."

"Here's death ta da head dat wears nae hair."

"Aft may we meet, an' never waar forn."

"Eerim skoorim, suntie voorim,
Oorim skaerim skaebo;
If onybody wis me skaed,
May ill beskae himsel', O."

In those days crews often fished together for many years, and the *foy* would occasionally take a devotional character, when some of the more emotional of the crew would recount with tear-bedimmed eyes the many providential deliverances of the past.

But when several members of the crew had fished in other boats, it was interesting to hear their tales of adventure, which were generally told with great minuteness. It may be of some little interest, especially in the use of our old words and sea phrases, to record a fisher's yarn over a drop of Hollands at a Lammas *foy*. The skipper was an oldish man, who had seen many a rough day at sea. His health had been drunk all round, and in reply he gave the following account of an experience at the *haf*. The narrative is given in his own words, in the dialect, and without any attempt at explaining the phrases he uses.

THE SKIPPER'S TALE.

"Boys, I'm no wirt ta carry noo, bit it's nae winder. Dir mony a saat watter drap gaen ower my head sin' da year '13, whin my midder wis left, an' I rowed in a fram boat my first year wi' aald Maans o' Buddabrake. I wis only saxteen, an' never been farder dan da lempit ebb an' da piltik eela, except a vaege or twa at da seats wi' Saidie o' Widwick.

"Weel, as I wis gaein' ta tell you, upo' aald Beltin Saturday Maans sends me

The Lammas Foy

wird ta come at da back o' da helly, hulan'-hulbaand, ta da lodge. Sae I sets me till an' drew ower da packie o' tows dat belanged ta mi faeder (soul be at rest), mended da gurdastörie o' my skalve, rax'd da tar ledder o' da grice for humbli-baands, bredged a pair o' skoags, an' sorted ae thing an' anidder.

"A' Sunday da wadder wis noo an' sae—a kind o' wasterly röd. I lays me doon brawly shön, sae as ta get a bluint o' sleep, bit dey wir a kind o' amp upo' me a' nicht, an' jöst aboot da swaar o' dim I waukens oot o' a dwaam an' looks i' da door. Da wind haed dauchin'd a guid dael, an' muggled 'im inta a stumba o' weet daag. Says I ta midder: 'Mam, rise dee wis up as shön as du can, an' mak' me some brakfast. I tink he's gaein' ta be sea wadder.'

"'Hadd di tongue, boy,' says shö; 'dis is only a slud atween wadders. Du'll better lay dee doon a peerie start, an' I'll creep me up an' kirn da tip o' milk, sae dat du gets a aer o' druttle i' da pig.'

Shetland Folk-Lore

"I lays me in ower da bed an' fa's upon a dwaam, an' I draems dat I wis gaein' i' da ebb alangst da banks o' da Hivda. I toucht dat I dang mi fit in a peerie toog, an' awa' I tumbled headicraw ower da banks. As I fell I felt a' in a vimmer, wi' a undömious yewk ower da sma' o' mi back. I lippens every moment ta faa among da caavies. Weel, wi' dat sam I sees a great muckle white fool comin' laavin in inonder me an' kaeps me upun her back. An' jöst as I wis being carried awa', the soond o' mam kirnin' an' da klaag o' wir klokkin flukner waukened me.

"Da sun wis noo come in trow wir ben lozen wi' a gludder dat wisna sma, sae I stramps furt, an' da first I meets is Tammy o' Nort'ouse. Says he: 'Boy, du's no sleepid sae lang as some o' wis. What tinks du o' 'im i' da' moarnin'?'

"'He's baith da w'ys laek,' says I. 'He's a pooshin wadder-head, a dirty söal i' da sea, an' I döna laek dis önd o' haet, wi' da öel risin' oot o' da grund. We'r a'

The Lammas Foy

seen a attrie mund comin' oot o' da laek o' dis.'

"'Du shörly minds eer-fern-yer,' says Tammy, 'aboot dis sam' time, whin da men o' Braken cam' vaan o' dir tows, an' wir nearly misförn takin' da String o' da Braagie.'

"'I mind dat weel enouch, an' fur my pairt, I widna gaeng oot ower da door da day, bit Maans sent me wird ta come ta da lodge—be-me-sang, sees du yon whillie rowin' ower da pöl. It's no anidder ene bit wir men comin', sae I'll awa' in an' mak' upo' me.'

"Whin I comes in my midder wis döne wi' kirnin'. Says shö: 'Boy, du wis in a roos whin du raise. Wha's yon du's been laugin wi'?' 'It wis Tammy o' da Nort'ouse. He's no gaein' aff da day.' 'Sae is he wise,' says mam. 'Dy ootgaein' 'ill gie me a sair haert, as mony a ene I'm haed afore. Bit Gude hadd His haand ower dee, an' sae I hoop He will.'

"I telt my midder da draem I haed

afore I raise, an' shö said: 'Believe du me du's gaein' ta hae trouble an' be in danger, bit du'll be broucht oot o' it a'. It's no ill ta draem aboot onything dat's white. Pairtin' wi' dee dis mornin' mak's da aald sair ta blöd—laess an' döl, da hidmaist oot-gaein' o' him dat belanged ta me is as vieve as da ooer dat I heard dat he wis nae mair.'

"Weel, I gets a' thing ready, an' awa' I gaengs ta da banks. Whin I comes inta da lodge, da skipper wis sittin' wi' a viskal o' gloy windin' fytlins fur da cappies. Robbie o' Vaaland an' Jockie o' Hamar wir repairin' da bink an sortin' da ringalodie, an' Henry o' Viggie wis sittin' wi' a yarkin alishen shodin' da rackie. Lowrie o' da Krö wis trampin' aboot da door, glowerin' i'ta da lift, seemin'ly in a ill-plaesed möd. Says da skipper ta me:

"'Boy, tak' dee wis da watter keg an' gaeng ta da green wal an' fill 'im, an' mind ta swill 'im oot.'

"'Whaar's da keg,' says I ta Lowrie.

"'He's lyin' afore da fiskafel i' da oost-room' o da sixern.'

"'Weel, awa' 'I gaengs an' fills da keg, an' lays 'im i' da shoormill. Noo, whin I comes in da skipper says :

"'Boys, I'll tell you what it is. I tink we'll try ta weet da tows, an' hae a set if it wis bit oot da lent o' da Vords. Da twar-tree piltiks i' da skjo ar noo faan upun, bit dey'll dö fir saide bliggs, an' it'll gaeng ill ta wark if we canna yaag twartree saide piltiks.'

"'Well,' says Lowrie, 'Gude guide dee, an' sae wis a', bit I'm no seen some o' you sae aaber whin hicher shines. Be-me-sang, der as vogerous follows as edder dee or me settin' da fit afore dem i' da moarnin'.'

"'Dat may be,' says Maans, 'bit I see you a' as graam an' as kibbie as I fir your pairt whin we come ashore. Sae, nae mair aboot it, bit lat wis draw doon, i' da name o' Gude.'

"Wi' dat every ene taks his buljaments an' awa' we gaengs ta da faar. Takin' frae da shords (da croon bane o' a whaal an' da röt o' a ragatree), we set wir backs till her, gettin' da eft drawil on a oak lin smeer'd wi' rotten droo, an' at da wird o' commaand frae Lowrie, whaa is takin' afore, we a' pu'd tagedder, an' doon shö cam' withoot ever makin' a stick.

"Lowrie, wha's saet wis eft upo' line-börd, jimps in ta stow da gear. Da packies o' tows wir first haandid in an' laid be-eft da oost-room fiskafel i' da shott. Da drink keg wis laid afore da baand. Da haandline reels were set i' da fore stammerin', an' da grind wi' da skoags, da skönes, an' da glaan wir a' laid i' da nabert locker i' da eft room. Every man noo took his place, set in his humbli-baand, an' laid oot his raemik. We turns da faar wi' da sun i' da richt coorse, an' dan da skipper says: 'Noo, boys, Gude hadd His haand aboot wis.'

"Very little wis spoken till we got oot da Nort' Soond, whin Lowrie wappit in his raemik an' stöd upo' da eft tilfer. Says

The Lammas Foy

he: 'Boys, if what's aboot 'im comes as he's laek, we'll shön hae a shange o' wind.'

"'Da carry is comin frae da nor'-wast,' says Jockie, 'an' if it hings up dat wy, it widna be a fairlie if he sood be maughtly troo da swaar o' da dim.'

"'Du says da carry is comin' frae da nor'-wast,' says Lowrie. 'Dat's a' da waar sign, fir, be-me-sang, he's sookin' till 'im. Onyene 'at haes een i' dir head can see dat dis only a loor atween wadders. We'll hae a ungastö afore sun-risin'.'

"'I döna laek yon önd alang da nort' banks,' says Jockie, 'an' dey wir ower monny brynics aboot 'im i' da moarnin' ta be lang guid.'

"Very little mair wis said till we cam' befram Vordadaal, whin Maans said dat we sood hadd better oot an' wast, till we got da Stack i' Slaggie an' da Daa at Stickie, an' dere hae a shot ta da boddim.

"'I never saw muckle guid dere,' says Lowrie. 'If we wir oot da lent o' da Stack at da Suilik an' da Ooverburg at da

Rönie, I widna say bit we wid get da grip o' da mamik, an' dan if dir ony saide i' da watter, we sood feel 'im dere.'

"Lowrie's plan wis taen, an' in a short time we wir at da seat. Maans an' Lowrie wir ta rin da boddim fir ling, an' Jockie an' Henry wir ta shut fir saide.

"'Haand me a kippok o' piltiks,' says Lowrie.

"'Be-ye-blithe,' says Robbie, 'no ene is in 'er.'

"We noo fan oot dat we haed left da bait piltiks i' da skjo. Da taen blamed ta tidder, till at lent Lowrie says: 'What's da öse o' irpin aboot a thing eence dat it's döne? Rex me da sköne an' glaan.'

"Lowrie noo pu's oot da lap o' his jūp an' snee'd aff a tivlik o' white claith. He fixed dis by da damp ta his saide heuk, an' haddin' up dis he spat upo' it, an' says 'Twee' as he shot da line an' beguid ta yaag. It wisna lang till he felt 'im, an' shön we haed plenty o' guid bait.

"'Noo, boys,' says Maans, 'we'll lay tö

The Lammas Foy

da sail an' hadd oot efter, an' by the time we'r da lent o' da Aald Grund, da aest tide 'ill be saagin.'

"Da wind wis noo blawin' a guid rinnin' frae da sooth-wast, sae by da time we haed snee'd da nabert an' aeten a bite o' bread, we wir at settin' grund. Da bow an' börop wir heaved owerbörd, an' Lowrie an' Jockie beguid ta set. By da time 'at da fort packie wis döne we haed ta shooinonder.

"'Haand me a cappie,' says Lowrie. 'da deil ae span gaengs mair oot ower her börd da nicht.'

"'I daarsay du's richt,' says Maans; 'he's no laek ta dauchin i' da stö.'

"'Du'll maybe ken dat er shö comes in,' replies Jockie, 'some o' wis is no sae vogerous for umplists o' dis kind.'

"By dis time we cuist da fraamer bow an' bent da vaarline. It noo took fower o' wis ta andow. Lowrie an' Robbie got on dir skin jups an' barmskins, an' made for hailin', bit juist as we wir lyin' till 'er, da vaarline bruke, an' da bow gaed doon wi' da russie o' da tide. We hanvayged aboot fir maistlins an ooer, bit never saw da bow again. We couldna shaa ae inch o' sail, da wind wis sae strong, an' nae weight i' da faar. We manned da raemiks an' set wis till her ta andow ahead. We rowed awa', seven lang an' seven short. Every noo an' dan shö wis takin' da green ludder in ower da forehead.

"Noo, whin we haed rowed until da turn o' da dim, Maans bids me gaeng awa' i' da forehead, an' look oot ower da waster side—'Fir wha kens,' says he, 'du'll maybe see da inner bow.'

"I wisna been lang till I toucht dat I saw da oomund o' sometin' i' da ask bewast wis. Rubbin' da saat watter oot o' my een, I tak's a guid look, an' ye'll no hinder me ta see da bow.

"'Dere shö is,' says I, 'a börop lent fram an' wast.'

"'Gude lat dee see a guid sight upo' dysel',' says Lowrie, 'pör aamis ting.'

The Lammas Foy

"We noo got hadd o' da bow, an' began ta hail. Da first dat comes ipo' da steid heuk wis a muckle skate. We wirna lang hailin', fir ye see we haed afore da wind. Da wadder wis sae dat we never wid tried her, haed it no been ta get some weight i' da boat, fir no ae oucht haed we bit twar-tree gaupins o' kleepie stanes.

"Whin we wir gottin in da tows, Maans toucht dat we sood close reef da sail an' lay da faar's head ta da aest'ard. Dis wis döne, bit pör sailin' we haed. Da spönd o' da sea gaed ower wis, an' it took twa o' wis—ene wi' a ouskerry an' ene wi' a fiddok—ta keep her wi' lee watter.

"We didna sail lang till we pat her aboot an' stöd ta wast'ard, wi' bow-kegs filled wi' saat watter an' da muckle skate hung ta da wadder kabe. We hadds at her a while; dan da ask lumed up an' we saw da kaavies. We haed da Holshyler at da Wilmer, an' da Stooraskord o' Widwick ower Fadaman's Stack.

"Da sea wis noo come ta dat 'at dey

wir nae livin ava. Maans wis headin' a lump, whin we never kens till da wadder raebaands made up an' da sail töre, an' noo dey wir naethin' fir it bit ta andow as lang as we wir able. Jockie haed a strae böddie, sae we ties da kappie stanes intil 'im an' rins 'im doon wi' da börops, an' what tink ye, it made a winderfil odds. It keepid wir head ta da wind. Da böddie wi' da sea bannocks wis a' weet, an' da bread wis in a sirpa.

"Weel, ta mak' a lang tale short, we andowed awa' laek dis till oot upo' da day, whin da rain hained an' da wind banged ta wast wi' a perfect gyndagooster.

"We noo hauls in wir fastie, an' rivs da sail wi' revatwirries an' set it upun her, an' awa' we gaengs wi' a bit o' sheet aff. We ran brawly weel till we wir crossin' da String o' da Braagie, whin a lump strack wis be-eft da shott an' carried awa' twa packies o' tows an' a half-a-score o' ling. Da boat wis filled ta da hadabaands, bit we dang da head oot o' da drink keg an'

The Lammas Foy

emptied her. Weel, as Gude wid hae it, we got safe ta da laand, juist whin da wives wis takkin' in da booriks.

"Wir ain folk haed been rinnin aboot da banks a' day, never tinkin' ta see wis again. Dat wis da sam' nicht 'at Rasmie o' Spraagatup an' his crew wis cassin awa' takin' da String o' da Röcok. Bit, Gude be tankit, it wis idderwise wi' wis fir dat time."

Also published by Llanerch:

A HANDBOOK OF THE
RUNIC MONUMENTS
OF BRITAIN AND
SCANDINAVIA
G Stevens

CORMAC THE SCALD
J W Collingwood

BANDAMANNA SAGA
John Porter

COUNTY FOLKLORE:
ORKNEY & SHETLAND
G F Black

BRITAIN'S LIVING
FOLKLORE
Roy Palmer

For a complete list of c300
titles, write to Llanerch Publishers,
Felinfach, Lampeter, Ceredigion, SA48 8PJ

INDEX

AABA KNOT, 26
Aaber heart wear, 156
Aamas bairns, 110
Aithsting, 29
Ask (haze), 133
Aurora, 116

BAAL WORSHIP, 90
Baldin, the (see halibut)
Balliasta, 28, 38, 92
Balta, 28
Battle axes, 66
Battles fought in Unst, 40
Benir, 99
Bergen (Norway), 22
Berg-grave, 48
Bersit o' Millaygue, 33
Bigtown, 100
Billy Brown, 217
Birds of omen, 20, 112, 163
Bismar, 62
Blaand, 133, 140
Blithe feast, 188
Blue Mull, 40, 41
Blue Mull, broch near, 46
Böddie, 53, 179
Boofell, 19
Borrowing Days, 117
Bressay, 89, 94
Bressay, sculptured stone, 94, 98
Brennya, Fladdabister, 69
Brettabister, 19
Brochs, the, 27, 28, 36, 41, 57
Brochs, finds in, 52
Brochs in Shetland, list of, 57
Brochs, usual sites of, 36, 57
Broch Holm, 51
Bronze brooches, 105, 106
Bronze weapons, 102
Broonies, 174, 180, 193

Brough, 28, 40
Brough Lodge (Fetlar), 51
Brough of Ness, 53
Brunthammarsland, 69
Bruntland, 69
Brynics, 115
Buggie, 132
Burgalea, 28
Burgasand, 28.
Burgascurs, 47
Burgawater, 28
Burial mounds, 27, 61, 78, 80, 85
Burra Isle, 89, 94
Burra, sculptured stone, 94
Burrafirth, 28, 38, 65, 153
Burrafirth, Noup of, 38
Burragarth, 28
Burraland, 28
Burravoe, 28
Burstin, 172, 189
Busta Standing Stone, 91
Byaena Sunday, 196

CANDLEMAS, 199
Castin' da clew, 191
Castin' da heart, 156
Cats, 113, 145
Catfirth, 44, 80
Catherine Tammasdaughter, 149
Cattle, diseases of, 163
Cattle, names given to, 176
Charms (see Spells)
Christenin' feasts, 188
Christmas, 196
Clibberswick, Unst, 105
Clickimin, Broch of, 57
Clivocast, 89
Cock, Superstitions regarding the, 165
Collister, 48

253

Index

Collingsbrough, 28
Colvidale, 28
Corncrake, 163
Cradle Songs, 180
Craigasoad, 32, 34
Cross Kirk, Braken, 101
Crucifell, 92
Culswick, 54
Cunningsburgh, 101
Cup holes, 32
Cupping, 159

DANCE MUSIC, 190
Delting, 19, 28
Dietary, 154, 177
Dratsie (the otter), 224
Drappin' Glasses, 190
Drift wood, 114
Dyes, 181, 195

EARTH HOUSES, Pictish, 37, 40
Eastness, Northmavine, 102
Easter, Broch of, 52
Elf-shot, 124, 144, 147, 151, 154
Eestik heads, 116
Eyrbyggja Saga, 86

FAIRIES, the (see Trows)
Fairies, utensils got from the, 166
Fairy knowes, 39
Fairy music, 151
Fastern's E'en, 199
Fathomin' the skroo, 192
Feasts, 187, 196
Fetlar, 18, 28
Feyness, 162, 165
Finns, the, 18, 26, 55
Finns, legends of the, 20
Finnigirt, 18
Finnie Knowe, Delting, 19
Finnie Knowe, Nesting, 19
Finnister, 18
Finnister dyke, 19
Finnister Hadds, 19
Fishing lines, 128
Fish liver, modes of cooking, 177
Fitful, 36
Fittin' feast, 188
Fivla, 39
Fivlagord, Hellyer o', 38
Fjelsmō, 131
Floki the Viking, 99
Footabrough, 28
Forker's Pig, 167
Foula, woods burned in, 70
Four-an'-twenty Day, 199

Fraam Gord, 149
Fraeklesgeo, 40
Funeral feasts, 189
Finnie (Funzie), 18
Fyall, 37

GAENFORE, 162
Games, 185, 189
Geirhild, 99
Giants, 91, 152
Gill o' Scraers, 47, 49
Girlsta, Loch of, 99
Gloy (laid straw), 171, 179
Gossabrough, 28
Grōliks, 189
Grunna Blaet, 176
Grunafirth, 19
Guddiks (riddles), 181, 190
Gulgraave o' da vyeadie, 143
Gulla Hammar, 152, 176
Gulsa (jaundice), 157
Gulsa whelk, 158
Gungsta, 166

HAF BOAT, 131, 135, 188
Haf fishing, 124
Hagmark an' da Rōcok, 130
Halibut, 22, 135, 205
Ha' o' Doon Helyer, 38
Hallowmas, 189
Haroldswick, 37
Heather beer, 34, 42
Helga Water, 160
Helly days, 196
Hellyers, 38, 40
Helyersmō, 131
Herculeson, John, 151
Herman the Giant, 152
Hermaness, 152
Herman's Ha', 152
Herman's Stack, 153
Heug an' da Rimble, 130
Heugins o' Watley, 123, 161
Hjokfinnie body, 26
Hole o' Henkie, 38
Holm of Burgawater, 53
Holy Fell (Iceland), 87
Hookame, Da Byre o', 43
Hoolin Brenda (Unst), 69
Hoolnamō, 131
Horns o' Haggmark, 153
Housifield, 37
Howdie, 144, 148, 154, 160, 165
Huggie-staff, 134

INFRANEB, 40

254

Index

JOHNSMAS, 90, 139, 188
Jube (the ocean), 118, 220

KAVEL-TREE, 134
Kirkatoon, 154
Klakaskurrs, 131
Knockin' stane, 29, 31, 78, 172
Kollie, 31, 62, 70, 156, 197
Krapp, Gulberwick, 69
Krös, sheep, 175
Kurkaby, Geo o', 47
Kurkaby, Noost o', 49

LAMMAS FOY, the, 235
Lamps, stone, 31
Lang Kame, 19
Lightnin' tree (lever of water mill), 174
Lucegrood, 33
Lund (Unst), 69
Lundawick, Broch Holm of, 46
Lunna Ness, 148
Lunnasting, 100, 104

MAAN'S RAITH, 130
Maron o' Nort'-a-Voe, 144
Meiths, 47, 130
Mills, hand, 171, 196
Mills, Shetland water, 172
Millya Gorda, 93
Milt token, 117
Moon brochs, 115
Moosie Gjo o' Straand, 217
Mort-caald, 157
Mother di, 119
Mound dwellers, 55
Mount Braa, Lerwick, 74
Mousa, Broch of, 54, 56
Muckle Hjoag, 81
Musselbrough (Unst), 28, 51

NADDOD the Viking, 99
Nesting, 18, 29, 38, 44, 45
Nesting Parish Church, broch near, 46
Neugle, the, 23, 174
Newgord, Ayre of, 47
Newgord Holm, 28
Nicker (see Neugle)
Nine mothers' maet, 94, 147, 156
Nippin Grund, 130
Nounsbrough, 54
Noralegs, 123, 141, 142, 145
Norseman, 35, 41, 55, 69, 70
Northmavine, 28
Norway, 18, 232
Norwick, 20, 37, 40, 153, 182

OGAM INSCRIPTIONS, 99, 100
Oganess, 28, 51
Omens, 93, 163
Ora, da, 23
Orkneys, the, 18
Outer Mull, 40
Overbrough, 28, 51

PAPA STOUR, 81, 91
Passin' da Harrow, 193
Pettafirth (Bressay), 43
Pettadale (Nesting), 43
Pettasmog, 43
Pettasmog, Den o', 38
Pettaster (Unst), 43
Pettawater, 43
Pettigarth (Whalsay), 43
Picking the mills, 155
Picts, the, 17, 27, 29, 35, 40, 41, 42, 50, 55, 63
Picts, mode of fishing, 32
Picts, means of livelihood of the, 29
Pictish place-names, 43
Pobies, the, of Unst, 132, 153
Prehistoric Remains, 61
Priest, murder of a, 161
Proverbs and Sayings, 203

QUERN, 171, 196

RAILSBROUGH, 28, 44
Rees (Quarff), 69
Rees (Buggle, Paece, Beltin), 116
Ribrendadelds (North Roe), 69
Riddles (see Guddiks)
Robbie Glen and the otter, 223
Rönies Hill, 91, 129, 153
Rora Klaet, 176
Runic Stones, 101

ST. NINIAN'S ISLE, 100
Safester, 81
Sandness, 29, 52, 101
Saxaford, 38
Saxe, the giant, 152
Scaw, 36, 40
Scotland, 17, 18, 232
Scraefield, 38
Scuddleswick, 38
Sea, descriptive terms, 119
Sea words, 121
Seals, 24
Seffster, Broch of, 54
Shaeks, 163
Sheep, colours of, 175
Sheep marks, 175, 176

Index

Shetland, first inhabitants of, 17, 27, 55
Siftin' siller, 193
Sixern, 124
Skerries, Battle Pund, 91
Skillister, Nesting, 89
Skjo, 177
Sköne, 111, 132, 134, 135
Skooin Brenda (Quarff), 69
Snaabrough, 28, 51
Snaaie heads, 115
Soapstone, 48, 49, 77, 79, 129
Social life, 169
Sounds made by animals, 164
Spells, 26, 142, 156, 158, 167, 168
Sprains, 159
Standing Stones, 27, 61, 89, 149
Stone Age, the, 62, 66
Stone axes, 45, 66
Stone axes, method of use, 68
Stone axes, perforated, 74
Stone axes, polished, 70
Stone circles, 91
Stone, domestic utensils of, 77
Stone implements, 63
Stone knives, 76
Stone lamp, 45, 78
Stones of Stennis, Orkney, 91
Stourbro' Hill, 53
Strandiebrough, 28, 51
Straw, articles made of, 195
Succamires, 89
Sumburgh, 29, 40
Superstitions, 93, 109, 126
Swarta Blaet, 176

TAMMAS' GRUND, 130
Tammasmas, 197
Three, the number, 188
Thunderbolts, 41, 66
Tirval's Seat, 130
Tivla, Rounds of, 93
Töfa, 170
Tongamö, 131
Torf Einar, 70
Toothache, 158
Trees in Shetland, 69
Trows, 18, 39, 43, 79, 88, 94, 122, 139, 143, 146, 148, 150, 155, 165, 166, 196

Tukkabersoada, 33
Tur-deil (beetle), 20
Turnin' the sleeve, 191
Tusker, 70
Tyin' the kale stock, 191

UNDERHOOL, 28, 30
Unst, 30, 40, 41, 152
Unst, brochs in, 28
Unst, stone circles, 92
Upstaander, 133, 188
Urns, 81
Uyasound, 28

VAARASOUND, 51
Vaarnakle, 129
Valafell, 48, 152
Venstrie, berg of, 93
Vestanore, 78
Viggie, 41
Vikings, 35, 43, 54
Vir, the, 50, 51
Virkie, the, 41
Virkie (Dunrossness), 51
Vivda (dried, unsalted meat), 189
Vords, the, 130

WADMIL, 195
Warts or Voards, 36
Wart o' Cleat (Whalsay), 148
Watsness (Walls), 64
Weather lore, 112
West Burrafirth, 54
Whales, 122
Whalsay, 29
Whalsay Man's Soliloquy, 178
Whinalea, 38
Whorls, 78
Wick o' Gröten, 150, 217
Wind, sea terms, 118
Winter Sunday, 113
Witches, 112, 122, 139, 196
Witchie-clock (beetle), 20
Woodwick, 28
Wormidale, 151

YELABRÖN, 160
Yell, 28
Yule, 196

THE END.